The Oxford Poetry Library

GENERAL EDITOR: FRANK KERMODE

GEORGE HERBERT (1593–1633), descendant of two eminent families on the border of Wales, began his career as Fellow and Public Orator at Cambridge. 'Setting foot into Divinity' as early as 1618, he gradually made his way, despite ill health, toward his ordination as priest of the Church of England, in 1630, when he became rector of the parish of Fuggleston-cum-Bemerton, near Salisbury. His book of poems, *The Temple* was published in 1633, some months after his death. His prose treatise, *The Country Parson*, did not appear until 1652. His poems met with immediate favour, and their popularity has continued up to the present day, when his reputation as poet is higher than at any time since the seventeenth century.

LOUIS L. MARTZ is retired Sterling Professor of English at Yale University. He is the author of five books on seventeenth-century poetry: *The Poetry of Meditation, The Paradise Within, The Wit of Love, Milton: Poet of Exile*, and *From Renaissance to Baroque*. He is co-editor of Thomas More's *Dialogue of Comfort* in the Yale edition of More's works. He has also written extensively on twentieth-century poetry and has edited both the *Collected Poems* and the *Selected Poems* of 'H.D.'.

FRANK KERMODE, retired King Edward VII Professor of English Literature at Cambridge, is the author of many books, including *Romantic Image, The Sense of an Ending, The Classic, The Genius of Secrecy, Forms of Attention*, and *History and Value*; he is also co-editor with John Hollander of *The Oxford Anthology of English Literature*.

THE OXFORD POETRY LIBRARY

GENERAL EDITOR: FRANK KERMODE

Matthew Arnold	*Miriam Allott*
William Blake	*Michael Mason*
Byron	*Jerome McGann*
Samuel Taylor Coleridge	*Heather Jackson*
John Dryden	*Keith Walker*
Thomas Hardy	*Samuel Hynes*
George Herbert	*Louis Martz*
Gerald Manley Hopkins	*Catherine Phillips*
Ben Jonson	*Ian Donaldson*
John Keats	*Elizabeth Cook*
Andrew Marvell	*Frank Kermode and Keith Walker*
John Milton	*Jonathan Goldberg and Stephen Orgel*
Alexander Pope	*Pat Rogers*
Sir Philip Sidney	*Katherine Duncan-Jones*
Henry Vaughan	*Louis Martz*
William Wordsworth	*Stephen Gill and Duncan Wu*

The Oxford Poetry Library

George Herbert

Edited by
LOUIS L. MARTZ

Oxford   New York
OXFORD UNIVERSITY PRESS
1994

Oxford University Press, Walton Street, Oxford OX2 6DP

Oxford New York Toronto
Delhi Bombay Calcutta Madras Karachi
Kuala Lumpur Singapore Hong Kong Tokyo
Nairobi Dar es Salaam Cape Town
Melbourne Auckland Madrid
and associated companies in
Berlin Ibadan

Oxford is a trade mark of Oxford University Press

This selection first published in the Oxford Poetry Library 1994

British Library Cataloguing in Publication Data
Data available

Library of Congress Cataloging in Publication Data
Herbert, George, 1593–1633.
[Poems. Selections]
George Herbert / edited by Louis L. Martz.
p.   cm.— (The Oxford poetry library)
Includes bibliographical references (p.).
I. Martz, Louis Lohr. II. Title. III. Series.
PR3507.A4   1994
821'.3—dc20   94–662
ISBN 0–19–282265–9

1 3 5 7 9 10 8 6 4 2

Typeset by J&L Composition Ltd, Filey, North Yorkshire
Printed in Great Britain by
Biddles Ltd
Guildford and King's Lynn

Contents

Chronology

	Nicholas Ferrar establishes his community at Little Gidding, Huntingdonshire.
1626	Herbert installed by proxy in the prebend of Leighton Ecclesia, with church at Leighton Bromswold, Huntingdonshire (his presence not required for this office).
1627	Herbert's mother dies; her memorial sermon delivered by John Donne: published along with Herbert's tribute in Latin and Greek verse, *Memoriae Matris Sacrum*.
1629	Marries Jane Danvers.
1630	26 April, installed as rector of the parish of Fuggleston-cum-Bemerton, Wiltshire, near Salisbury.
	19 September, ordained priest in Salisbury Cathedral.
1631	John Donne dies.
1633	1 March, Herbert dies; burial in Bemerton church.
	The Temple published at Cambridge, under the supervision of Nicholas Ferrar.
	First edition of Donne's *Poems* published.
1652	*Herbert's Remains* published, including *The Country Parson*.

Note on the Text

The present volume includes all the poems of *The Temple*, except for the long, and apparently early poem, *The Church Militant*, which in the first edition of 1633 follows *The Church*, a section marked 'Finis' after the final poem, 'Love' (III). In the manuscript now in Dr Williams's Library, London, the word 'Finis' also occurs after 'Love' (III), and then five blank pages intervene before *The Church Militant*, an indication that Herbert may have regarded the poem as a separate piece. Similarly, in the Williams manuscript, four blank pages intervene between *The Church Militant* and Herbert's Latin poems. The addition of the long poem after *The Church* may represent a decision by Nicholas Ferrar, who edited *1633*.

The modernized text here presented is based upon the old-spelling text provided in the edition of Herbert's *Works* edited by F. E. Hutchinson (Oxford: Clarendon Press, 1941). Here and there old forms and spellings have been retained for special reasons of meaning and sound, and a few readings have been adopted from the complete Bodleian manuscript of Herbert's poems and from the early Williams manuscript, which contains only sixty-nine of the 164 poems in *The Temple*, plus six poems that were not included in the final version. The punctuation, in accord with the practice of F. E. Hutchinson, generally follows that of the first edition, with alterations made in cases of obscurity or excessive use of commas. Numbers in parentheses after titles are editorial additions.

THE TEMPLE

Sacred Poems
and
Private Ejaculations

The Dedication

Lord, my first fruits present themselves to thee;
Yet not mine neither: for from thee they came,
And must return. Accept of them and me,
And make us strive, who shall sing best thy name.
   Turn their eyes hither, who shall make a gain:
    Theirs, who shall hurt themselves or me, refrain.

THE CHURCH-PORCH

Perirrhanterium

1

Thou, whose sweet youth and early hopes enhance
Thy rate and price, and mark thee for a treasure;
Hearken unto a verser, who may chance
Rhyme thee to good, and make a bait of pleasure.
 A verse may find him, who a sermon flies,
 And turn delight into a sacrifice.

2

Beware of lust: it doth pollute and foul
Whom God in Baptism washed with his own blood.
It blots thy lesson written in thy soul;
The holy lines cannot be understood.   10
 How dare those eyes upon a Bible look,
 Much less towards God, whose lust is all their book?

3

Abstain wholly, or wed. Thy bounteous Lord
Allows thee choice of paths: take no by-ways;
But gladly welcome what he doth afford;
Not grudging, that thy lust hath bounds and stays.
 Continence hath his joy: weigh both; and so
 If rottenness have more, let Heaven go.

4

If God had laid all common, certainly
Man would have been th' incloser: but since now 20
God hath impaled us, on the contrary
Man breaks the fence, and every ground will plough.
 O what were man, might he himself misplace!
 Sure to be cross he would shift feet and face.

5

Drink not the third glass, which thou canst not tame,
When once it is within thee, but before
Mayst rule it, as thou list; and pour the shame,
Which it would pour on thee, upon the floor.
   It is most just to throw that on the ground,
    Which would throw me there, if I keep the round.   30

6

He that is drunken, may his mother kill
Big with his sister: he hath lost the reins,
Is outlawed by himself: all kind of ill
Did with his liquor slide into his veins.
   The drunkard forfeits Man, and doth devest
    All worldly right, save what he hath by beast.

7

Shall I, to please another's wine-sprung mind,
Lose all mine own? God hath giv'n me a measure
Short of his can and body; must I find
A pain in that, wherein he finds a pleasure?   40
   Stay at the third glass: if thou lose thy hold,
    Then thou art modest, and the wine grows bold.

8

If reason move not gallants, quit the room,
(All in a shipwrack shift their several way)
Let not a common ruin thee intomb:
Be not a beast in courtesy; but stay,
   Stay at the third cup, or forgo the place.
    Wine above all things doth God's stamp deface.

9

Yet, if thou sin in wine or wantonness,
Boast not thereof; nor make thy shame thy glory.   50
Frailty gets pardon by submissiveness;
But he that boasts, shuts that out of his story.
   He makes flat war with God, and doth defy
    With his poor clod of earth the spacious sky.

10

Take not his name, who made thy mouth, in vain:
It gets thee nothing, and hath no excuse.
Lust and wine plead a pleasure, avarice gain:
But the cheap swearer through his open sluice
  Lets his soul run for nought, as little fearing.
  Were I an Epicure, I could bate swearing.   60

11

When thou dost tell another's jest, therein
Omit the oaths, which true wit cannot need:
Pick out of tales the mirth, but not the sin.
He pares his apple, that will cleanly feed.
  Play not away the virtue of that name,
  Which is thy best stake, when griefs make thee tame.

12

The cheapest sins most dearly punished are;
Because to shun them also is so cheap:
For we have wit to mark them, and to spare.
O crumble not away thy soul's fair heap.   70
  If thou wilt die, the gates of hell are broad:
  Pride and full sins have made the way a road.

13

Lie not; but let thy heart be true to God,
Thy mouth to it, thy actions to them both:
Cowards tell lies, and those that fear the rod;
The stormy working soul spits lies and froth.
  Dare to be true. Nothing can need a lie:
  A fault, which needs it most, grows two thereby.

14

Fly idleness, which yet thou canst not fly
By dressing, mistressing, and compliment.   80
If those take up thy day, the sun will cry
Against thee: for his light was only lent.
  God gave thy soul brave wings; put not those feathers
  Into a bed, to sleep out all ill weathers.

15

Art thou a magistrate? then be severe:
If studious, copy fair what time hath blurred;
Redeem truth from his jaws: if soldier,
Chase brave employments with a naked sword
   Throughout the world. Fool not: for all may have,
   If they dare try, a glorious life, or grave.   90

16

O England! full of sin, but most of sloth;
Spit out thy phlegm, and fill thy breast with glory:
Thy gentry bleats, as if thy native cloth
Transfused a sheepishness into thy story:
   Not that they all are so; but that the most
   Are gone to grass, and in the pasture lost.

17

This loss springs chiefly from our education.
Some till their ground, but let weeds choke their son:
Some mark a partridge, never their child's fashion:
Some ship them over, and the thing is done.   100
   Study this art, make it thy great design;
   And if God's image move thee not, let thine.

18

Some great estates provide, but do not breed
A mast'ring mind; so both are lost thereby:
Or else they breed them tender, make them need
All that they leave: this is flat poverty.
   For he, that needs five thousand pound to live,
   Is full as poor as he, that needs but five.

19

The way to make thy son rich is to fill
His mind with rest, before his trunk with riches: 110
For wealth without contentment climbs a hill
To feel those tempests, which fly over ditches.
   But if thy son can make ten pound his measure,
   Then all thou addest may be called his treasure.

20

When thou dost purpose aught within thy power,
Be sure to do it, though it be but small:
Constancy knits the bones, and makes us stour,
When wanton pleasures beckon us to thrall.
    Who breaks his own bond, forfeiteth himself:
    What nature made a ship, he makes a shelf.   120

21

Do all things like a man, not sneakingly:
Think the king sees thee still; for his King does.
Simp'ring is but a lay-hypocrisy:
Give it a corner, and the clue undoes.
    Who fears to do ill, sets himself to task:
    Who fears to do well, sure should wear a mask.

22

Look to thy mouth; diseases enter there.
Thou hast two sconces, if thy stomach call;
Carve, or discourse; do not a famine fear.
Who carves, is kind to two; who talks, to all.   130
    Look on meat, think it dirt, then eat a bit;
    And say withal, Earth to earth I commit.

23

Slight those who say amidst their sickly healths,
Thou liv'st by rule. What doth not so, but man?
Houses are built by rule, and commonwealths.
Entice the trusty sun, if that thou can,
    From his ecliptic line: beckon the sky.
    Who lives by rule then, keeps good company.

24

Who keeps no guard upon himself, is slack,
And rots to nothing at the next great thaw.   140
Man is a shop of rules, a well trussed pack,
Whose every parcel underwrites a law.
    Lose not thyself, nor give thy humours way:
    God gave them to thee under lock and key.

25

By all means use sometimes to be alone.
Salute thyself: see what thy soul doth wear.
Dare to look in thy chest, for 'tis thine own:
And tumble up and down what thou find'st there.
   Who cannot rest till he good fellows find,
   He breaks up house, turns out of doors his mind.   150

26

Be thrifty, but not covetous: therefore give
Thy need, thine honour, and thy friend his due.
Never was scraper brave man. Get to live;
Then live, and use it: else, it is not true
   That thou hast gotten. Surely use alone
   Makes money not a contemptible stone.

27

Never exceed thy income. Youth may make
Ev'n with the year: but age, if it will hit,
Shoots a bow short, and lessens still his stake,
As the day lessens, and his life with it.   160
   Thy children, kindred, friends upon thee call;
   Before thy journey fairly part with all.

28

Yet in thy thriving still misdoubt some evil;
Lest gaining gain on thee, and make thee dim
To all things else. Wealth is the conjurer's devil;
Whom when he thinks he hath, the devil hath him.
   Gold thou mayst safely touch; but if it stick
   Unto thy hands, it woundeth to the quick.

29

What skills it, if a bag of stones or gold
About thy neck do drown thee? raise thy head;   170
Take stars for money; stars not to be told
By any art, yet to be purchased.
   None is so wasteful as the scraping dame,
   She loseth three for one; her soul, rest, fame.

30

By no means run in debt: take thine own measure.
Who cannot live on twenty pound a year,
Cannot on forty: he's a man of pleasure,
A kind of thing that's for itself too dear.
  The curious unthrift makes his clothes too wide,
  And spares himself, but would his tailor chide. 180

31

Spend not on hopes. They that by pleading clothes
Do fortunes seek, when worth and service fail,
Would have their tale believèd for their oaths,
And are like empty vessels under sail.
  Old courtiers know this; therefore set out so,
  As all the day thou mayst hold out to go.

32

In clothes, cheap handsomeness doth bear the bell.
Wisdom's a trimmer thing than shop e'er gave.
Say not then, This with that lace will do well;
But, This with my discretion will be brave. 190
  Much curiousness is a perpetual wooing,
  Nothing with labour, folly long a-doing.

33

Play not for gain, but sport. Who plays for more
Than he can lose with pleasure, stakes his heart;
Perhaps his wife's too, and whom she hath bore:
Servants and churches also play their part.
  Only a herald, who that way doth pass,
  Finds his cracked name at length in the church glass.

34

If yet thou love game at so dear a rate,
Learn this, that hath old gamesters dearly cost: 200
Dost lose? rise up: dost win? rise in that state.
Who strive to sit out losing hands, are lost.
  Game is a civil gunpowder, in peace
  Blowing up houses with their whole increase.

35

In conversation boldness now bears sway.
But know, that nothing can so foolish be,
As empty boldness: therefore first assay
To stuff thy mind with solid bravery;
   Then march on gallant: get substantial worth.
   Boldness gilds finely, and will set it forth.   210

36

Be sweet to all. Is thy complexion sour?
Then keep such company; make them thy allay:
Get a sharp wife, a servant that will lour.
A stumbler stumbles least in rugged way.
   Command thyself in chief. He life's war knows,
   Whom all his passions follow, as he goes.

37

Catch not at quarrels. He that dares not speak
Plainly and home, is coward of the two.
Think not thy fame at ev'ry twitch will break:
By great deeds show, that thou canst little do;   220
   And do them not: that shall thy wisdom be;
   And change thy temperance into bravery.

38

If that thy fame with ev'ry toy be posed,
'Tis a thin web, which poisonous fancies make:
But the great soldier's honour was composed
Of thicker stuff, which would endure a shake.
   Wisdom picks friends; civility plays the rest.
   A toy shunned cleanly passeth with the best.

39

Laugh not too much: the witty man laughs least:
For wit is news only to ignorance.   230
Less at thine own things laugh; lest in the jest
Thy person share, and the conceit advance.
   Make not thy sport, abuses: for the fly
   That feeds on dung, is colourèd thereby.

40

Pick out of mirth, like stones out of thy ground,
Profaneness, filthiness, abusiveness.
These are the scum, with which coarse wits abound:
The fine may spare these well, yet not go less.
 All things are big with jest: nothing that's plain,
 But may be witty, if thou hast the vein.   240

41

Wit's an unruly engine, wildly striking
Sometimes a friend, sometimes the engineer.
Hast thou the knack? pamper it not with liking:
But if thou want it, buy it not too dear.
 Many, affecting wit beyond their power,
 Have got to be a dear fool for an hour.

42

A sad wise valour is the brave complexion,
That leads the van, and swallows up the cities.
The giggler is a milk-maid, whom infection
Or a fired beacon frighteth from his ditties.   250
 Then he's the sport: the mirth then in him rests,
 And the sad man is cock of all his jests.

43

Towards great persons use respective boldness:
That temper gives them theirs, and yet doth take
Nothing from thine: in service, care or coldness
Doth rateably thy fortunes mar or make.
 Feed no man in his sins: for adulation
 Doth make thee parcel-devil in damnation.

44

Envy not greatness: for thou mak'st thereby
Thyself the worse, and so the distance greater.   260
Be not thine own worm: yet such jealousy,
As hurts not others, but may make thee better,
 Is a good spur. Correct thy passions' spite;
 Then may the beasts draw thee to happy light.

45

When baseness is exalted, do not bate
The place its honour, for the person's sake.
The shrine is that which thou dost venerate,
And not the beast, that bears it on his back.
  I care not though the cloth of state should be
  Not of rich arras, but mean tapestry.   270

46

Thy friend put in thy bosom: wear his eyes
Still in thy heart, that he may see what's there.
If cause require, thou art his sacrifice;
Thy drops of blood must pay down all his fear:
  But love is lost, the way of friendship's gone,
  Though David had his Jonathan, Christ his John.

47

Yet be not surety, if thou be a father.
Love is a personal debt. I cannot give
My children's right, nor ought he take it: rather
Both friends should die, than hinder them to live.   280
  Fathers first enter bonds to nature's ends;
  And are her sureties, ere they are a friend's.

48

If thou be single, all thy goods and ground
Submit to love; but yet not more than all.
Give one estate, as one life. None is bound
To work for two, who brought himself to thrall.
  God made me one man; love makes me no more,
  Till labour come, and make my weakness score.

49

In thy discourse, if thou desire to please,
All such is courteous, useful, new, or witty.   290
Usefulness comes by labour, wit by ease;
Courtesy grows in court; news in the city.
  Get a good stock of these, then draw the card
  That suits him best, of whom thy speech is heard.

50

Entice all neatly to what they know best;
For so thou dost thyself and him a pleasure:
(But a proud ignorance will lose his rest,
Rather than show his cards.) Steal from his treasure
 What to ask further. Doubts well raised do lock
 The speaker to thee, and preserve thy stock.   300

51

If thou be master-gunner, spend not all
That thou canst speak, at once; but husband it,
And give men turns of speech: do not forestall
By lavishness thine own, and others' wit,
 As if thou mad'st thy will. A civil guest
 Will no more talk all, than eat all the feast.

52

Be calm in arguing: for fierceness makes
Error a fault, and truth discourtesy.
Why should I feel another man's mistakes
More than his sicknesses or poverty?   310
 In love I should: but anger is not love,
 Nor wisdom neither: therefore gently move.

53

Calmness is great advantage: he that lets
Another chafe, may warm him at his fire,
Mark all his wand'rings, and enjoy his frets;
As cunning fencers suffer heat to tire.
 Truth dwells not in the clouds: the bow that's there
 Doth often aim at, never hit the sphere.

54

Mark what another says: for many are
Full of themselves, and answer their own notion. 320
Take all into thee; then with equal care
Balance each dram of reason, like a potion.
 If truth be with thy friend, be with them both:
 Share in the conquest, and confess a troth.

55

Be useful where thou livest, that they may
Both want and wish thy pleasing presence still.
Kindness, good parts, great places are the way
To compass this. Find out men's wants and will,
    And meet them there. All worldly joys go less
    To the one joy of doing kindnesses.   330

56

Pitch thy behaviour low, thy projects high;
So shalt thou humble and magnanimous be:
Sink not in spirit: who aimeth at the sky,
Shoots higher much than he that means a tree.
    A grain of glory mixed with humbleness
    Cures both a fever and lethargicness.

57

Let thy mind still be bent, still plotting where,
And when, and how the business may be done.
Slackness breeds worms; but the sure traveller,
Though he alight sometimes, still goeth on.   340
    Active and stirring spirits live alone.
    Write on the others, Here lies such a one.

58

Slight not the smallest loss, whether it be
In love or honour: take account of all;
Shine like the sun in every corner: see
Whether thy stock of credit swell, or fall.
    Who say, I care not, those I give for lost;
    And to instruct them, will not quit the cost.

59

Scorn no man's love, though of a mean degree;
Love is a present for a mighty king.   350
Much less make anyone thy enemy.
As guns destroy, so may a little sling.
    The cunning workman never doth refuse
    The meanest tool, that he may chance to use.

60

All foreign wisdom doth amount to this,
To take all that is given; whether wealth,
Or love, or language; nothing comes amiss:
A good digestion turneth all to health:
  And then as far as fair behaviour may,
  Strike off all scores; none are so clear as they.   360

61

Keep all thy native good, and naturalize
All foreign of that name; but scorn their ill:
Embrace their activeness, not vanities.
Who follows all things, forfeiteth his will.
  If thou observest strangers in each fit,
  In time they'll run thee out of all thy wit.

62

Affect in things about thee cleanliness,
That all may gladly board thee, as a flower.
Slovens take up their stock of noisomeness
Beforehand, and anticipate their last hour.   370
  Let thy mind's sweetness have his operation
  Upon thy body, clothes, and habitation.

63

In alms regard thy means, and others' merit.
Think heav'n a better bargain, than to give
Only thy single market-money for it.
Join hands with God to make a man to live.
  Give to all something; to a good poor man,
  Till thou change names, and be where he began.

64

Man is God's image; but a poor man is
Christ's stamp to boot: both images regard.   380
God reckons for him, counts the favour his:
Write, So much giv'n to God; thou shalt be heard.
  Let thy alms go before, and keep heav'ns gate
  Open for thee; or both may come too late.

65

Restore to God his due in tithe and time:
A tithe purloined cankers the whole estate.
Sundays observe: think when the bells do chime,
'Tis angels' music; therefore come not late.
  God then deals blessings: if a king did so,
  Who would not haste, nay give, to see the show?   390

66

Twice on the day his due is understood;
For all the week thy food so oft he gave thee.
Thy cheer is mended; bate not of the food,
Because 'tis better, and perhaps may save thee.
  Thwart not the Mighty God: O be not cross.
  Fast when thou wilt but then, 'tis gain not loss.

67

Though private prayer be a brave design,
Yet public hath more promises, more love:
And love's a weight to hearts, to eyes a sign.
We all are but cold suitors; let us move   400
  Where it is warmest. Leave thy six and seven;
  Pray with the most: for where most pray, is heaven.

68

When once thy foot enters the church, be bare.
God is more there, than thou: for thou art there
Only by his permission. Then beware,
And make thyself all reverence and fear.
  Kneeling ne'er spoiled silk stocking: quit thy state.
  All equal are within the church's gate.

69

Resort to sermons, but to prayers most:
Praying's the end of preaching. O be dressed;   410
Stay not for th' other pin: why, thou hast lost
A joy for it worth worlds. Thus hell doth jest
  Away thy blessings, and extremely flout thee,
  Thy clothes being fast, but thy soul loose about thee.

70

In time of service seal up both thine eyes,
And send them to thine heart; that spying sin,
They may weep out the stains by them did rise:
Those doors being shut, all by the ear comes in.
 Who marks in church-time others' symmetry,
 Makes all their beauty his deformity.

420

71

Let vain or busy thoughts have there no part:
Bring not thy plough, thy plots, thy pleasures thither.
Christ purged his temple; so must thou thy heart.
All worldly thoughts are but thieves met together
 To cozen thee. Look to thy actions well:
 For churches are either our heav'n or hell.

72

Judge not the preacher; for he is thy judge:
If thou mislike him, thou conceiv'st him not.
God calleth preaching folly. Do not grudge
To pick out treasures from an earthen pot.

430

 The worst speak something good: if all want sense,
 God takes a text, and preacheth patience.

73

He that gets patience, and the blessing which
Preachers conclude with, hath not lost his pains.
He that by being at church escapes the ditch,
Which he might fall in by companions, gains.
 He that loves God's abode, and to combine
 With saints on earth, shall one day with them shine.

74

Jest not at preachers' language, or expression:
How know'st thou, but thy sins made him miscarry?

440

Then turn thy faults and his into confession:
God sent him, whatsoe'er he be: O tarry,
 And love him for his Master: his condition,
 Though it be ill, makes him no ill physician.

75

None shall in hell such bitter pangs endure,
As those, who mock at God's way of salvation.
Whom oil and balsams kill, what salve can cure?
They drink with greediness a full damnation.
 The Jews refusèd thunder; and we, folly.
 Though God do hedge us in, yet who is holy? 450

76

Sum up at night, what thou hast done by day;
And in the morning, what thou hast to do.
Dress and undress thy soul: mark the decay
And growth of it: if with thy watch, that too
 Be down, then wind up both; since we shall be
 Most surely judged, make thy accounts agree.

77

In brief, acquit thee bravely; play the man.
Look not on pleasures as they come, but go.
Defer not the least virtue: life's poor span
Make not an ell, by trifling in thy woe. 460
 If thou do ill; the joy fades, not the pains:
 If well; the pain doth fade, the joy remains.

Superliminare

Thou, whom the former precepts have
Sprinkled and taught, how to behave
Thyself in church; approach, and taste
The church's mystical repast.

———————

Avoid, profaneness; come not here:
Nothing but holy, pure, and clear,
Or that which groaneth to be so,
May at his peril further go.

THE CHURCH

The Altar

A broken ALTAR, Lord, thy servant rears,
Made of a heart, and cemented with tears:
  Whose parts are as thy hand did frame;
  No workman's tool hath touched the same.
        A   HEART   alone
        Is   such   a   stone,
        As   nothing   but
        Thy pow'r doth cut.
        Wherefore each part
        Of my hard heart
        Meets in this frame,
        To praise thy Name:
  That, if I chance to hold my peace,
  These stones to praise thee may not cease.
O let thy blessed SACRIFICE be mine,
And sanctify this ALTAR to be thine.

The Sacrifice

Oh all ye, who pass by, whose eyes and mind
To worldly things are sharp, but to me blind;
To me, who took eyes that I might you find:
               Was ever grief like mine?

The princes of my people make a head
Against their Maker: they do wish me dead,
Who cannot wish, except I give them bread:
               Was ever grief like mine?

Without me each one, who doth now me brave,
Had to this day been an Egyptian slave.
They use that power against me, which I gave:
               Was ever grief like mine?

Mine own apostle, who the bag did bear,
Though he had all I had, did not forbear
To sell me also, and to put me there:
     Was ever grief like mine?

For thirty pence he did my death devise,
Who at three hundred did the ointment prize,
Not half so sweet as my sweet sacrifice:
     Was ever grief like mine?   20

Therefore my soul melts, and my heart's dear treasure
Drops blood (the only beads) my words to measure:
O let this cup pass, if it be thy pleasure:
     Was ever grief like mine?

These drops being tempered with a sinner's tears
A balsam are for both the hemispheres:
Curing all wounds, but mine; all, but my fears:
     Was ever grief like mine?

Yet my disciples sleep: I cannot gain
One hour of watching; but their drowsy brain   30
Comforts not me, and doth my doctrine stain:
     Was ever grief like mine?

Arise, arise, they come. Look how they run!
Alas! what haste they make to be undone!
How with their lanterns do they seek the sun!
     Was ever grief like mine?

With clubs and staves they seek me, as a thief,
Who am the Way and Truth, the true relief;
Most true to those, who are my greatest grief:
     Was ever grief like mine?   40

Judas, dost thou betray me with a kiss?
Canst thou find hell about my lips? and miss
Of life, just at the gates of life and bliss?
     Was ever grief like mine?

See, they lay hold on me, not with the hands
Of faith, but fury: yet at their commands
I suffer binding, who have loosed their bands:
                Was ever grief like mine?

All my disciples fly; fear puts a bar
Betwixt my friends and me. They leave the star,   50
That brought the wise men of the East from far.
                Was ever grief like mine?

Then from one ruler to another bound
They lead me; urging, that it was not sound
What I taught: comments would the text confound.
                Was ever grief like mine?

The priest and rulers all false witness seek
'Gainst him, who seeks not life, but is the meek
And ready Paschal Lamb of this great week:
                Was ever grief like mine?   60

Then they accuse me of great blasphemy,
That I did thrust into the Deity,
Who never thought that any robbery:
                Was ever grief like mine?

Some said, that I the Temple to the floor
In three days razed, and raisèd as before.
Why, he that built the world can do much more:
                Was ever grief like mine?

Then they condemn me all with that same breath,
Which I do give them daily, unto death.   70
Thus Adam my first breathing rendereth:
                Was ever grief like mine?

They bind, and lead me unto Herod: he
Sends me to Pilate. This makes them agree;
But yet their friendship is my enmity:
                Was ever grief like mine?

Herod and all his bands do set me light,
Who teach all hands to war, fingers to fight,
And only am the Lord of Hosts and might:
                    Was ever grief like mine?   80

Herod in judgement sits, while I do stand;
Examines me with a censorious hand:
I him obey, who all things else command:
                    Was ever grief like mine?

The Jews accuse me with despitefulness;
And vying malice with my gentleness,
Pick quarrels with their only happiness:
                    Was ever grief like mine?

I answer nothing, but with patience prove
If stony hearts will melt with gentle love.   90
But who does hawk at eagles with a dove?
                    Was ever grief like mine?

My silence rather doth augment their cry;
My dove doth back into my bosom fly,
Because the raging waters still are high:
                    Was ever grief like mine?

Heark how they cry aloud still, *Crucify*:
It is not fit he live a day, they cry,
Who cannot live less than eternally:
                    Was ever grief like mine?   100

Pilate, a stranger, holdeth off; but they,
Mine own dear people, cry, *Away*, *away*,
With noises confusèd frighting the day:
                    Was ever grief like mine?

Yet still they shout, and cry, and stop their ears,
Putting my life among their sins and fears,
And therefore wish *my blood on them and theirs*:
                    Was ever grief like mine?

See how spite cankers things. These words aright
Usèd, and wishèd, are the whole world's light: 110
But honey is their gall, brightness their night:
     Was ever grief like mine?

They choose a murderer, and all agree
In him to do themselves a courtesy:
For it was their own case who killèd me:
     Was ever grief like mine?

And a seditious murderer he was:
But I the Prince of peace; peace that doth pass
All understanding, more than heav'n doth glass:
     Was ever grief like mine?   120

Why, Caesar is their only king, not I:
He clave the stony rock, when they were dry;
But surely not their hearts, as I well try:
     Was ever grief like mine?

Ah! how they scourge me! yet my tenderness
Doubles each lash: and yet their bitterness
Winds up my grief to a mysteriousness:
     Was ever grief like mine?

They buffet him, and box him as they list,
Who grasps the earth and heaven with his fist,   130
And never yet, whom he would punish, missed:
     Was ever grief like mine?

Behold, they spit on me in scornful wise,
Who by my spittle gave the blind man eyes,
Leaving his blindness to my enemies:
     Was ever grief like mine?

My face they cover, though it be divine.
As Moses' face was veilèd, so is mine,
Lest on their double-dark souls either shine:
     Was ever grief like mine?   140

Servants and abjects flout me; they are witty:
Now prophesy who strikes thee, is their ditty.
So they in me deny themselves all pity:
            Was ever grief like mine?

And now I am delivered unto death,
Which each one calls for so with utmost breath,
That he before me well nigh suffereth:
            Was ever grief like mine?

Weep not, dear friends, since I for both have wept
When all my tears were blood, the while you slept: 150
Your tears for your own fortunes should be kept:
            Was ever grief like mine?

The soldiers lead me to the common hall;
There they deride me, they abuse me all:
Yet for twelve heav'nly legions I could call:
            Was ever grief like mine?

Then with a scarlet robe they me array;
Which shows my blood to be the only way
And cordial left to repair man's decay:
            Was ever grief like mine?   160

Then on my head a crown of thorns I wear:
For these are all the grapes Sion doth bear,
Though I my vine planted and watered there:
            Was ever grief like mine?

So sits the earth's great curse in Adam's fall
Upon my head: so I remove it all
From th' earth unto my brows, and bear the thrall:
            Was ever grief like mine?

Then with the reed they gave to me before,
They strike my head, the rock from whence all store   170
Of heav'nly blessings issue evermore:
            Was ever grief like mine?

They bow their knees to me, and cry, *Hail king*:
Whatever scoffs and scornfulness can bring,
I am the floor, the sink, where they it fling:
                    Was ever grief like mine?

Yet since man's sceptres are as frail as reeds,
And thorny all their crowns, bloody their weeds;
I, who am Truth, turn into truth their deeds:
                    Was ever grief like mine?   180

The soldiers also spit upon that face,
Which angels did desire to have the grace,
And prophets, once to see, but found no place:
                    Was ever grief like mine?

Thus trimmèd, forth they bring me to the rout,
Who *Crucify him*, cry with one strong shout.
God holds his peace at man, and man cries out:
                    Was ever grief like mine?

They lead me in once more, and putting then
Mine own clothes on, they lead me out again.   190
Whom devils fly, thus is he tossed of men:
                    Was ever grief like mine?

And now weary of sport, glad to engross
All spite in one, counting my life their loss,
They carry me to my most bitter cross:
                    Was ever grief like mine?

My cross I bear myself, until I faint:
Then Simon bears it for me by constraint,
The decreed burden of each mortal Saint:
                    Was ever grief like mine?   200

O all ye who pass by, behold and see;
Man stole the fruit, but I must climb the tree;
The tree of life to all, but only me:
                    Was ever grief like mine?

Lo, here I hang, charged with a world of sin,
The greater world o' th' two; for that came in
By words, but this by sorrow I must win:
                         Was ever grief like mine?

Such sorrow as, if sinful man could feel,
Or feel his part, he would not cease to kneel,   210
Till all were melted, though he were all steel:
                         Was ever grief like mine?

But, *O my God, my God!* why leav'st thou me,
The son, in whom thou dost delight to be?
My God, my God—
                         Never was grief like mine.

Shame tears my soul, my body many a wound;
Sharp nails pierce this, but sharper that confound;
Reproaches, which are free, while I am bound.
                         Was ever grief like mine?   220

Now heal thyself, physician; now come down.
Alas! I did so, when I left my crown
And father's smile for you, to feel his frown:
                         Was ever grief like mine?

In healing not myself, there doth consist
All that salvation, which ye now resist;
Your safety in my sickness doth subsist:
                         Was ever grief like mine?

Betwixt two thieves I spend my utmost breath,
As he that for some robbery suffereth.   230
Alas! what have I stolen from you? Death.
                         Was ever grief like mine?

A king my title is, prefixed on high;
Yet by my subjects am condemned to die
A servile death in servile company:
                         Was ever grief like mine?

They give me vinegar mingled with gall,
But more with malice: yet, when they did call,
With manna, angels' food, I fed them all:
                 Was ever grief like mine?   240

They part my garments, and by lot dispose
My coat, the type of love, which once cured those
Who sought for help, never malicious foes:
                 Was ever grief like mine?

Nay, after death their spite shall further go;
For they will pierce my side, I full well know;
That as sin came, so Sacraments might flow:
                 Was ever grief like mine?

But now I die; now all is finishèd.
My woe, man's weal: and now I bow my head.   250
Only let others say, when I am dead,
                 Never was grief like mine.

The Thanksgiving

Oh King of grief! (a title strange, yet true,
   To thee of all kings only due)
Oh King of wounds! how shall I grieve for thee,
   Who in all grief preventest me?
Shall I weep blood? why, thou hast wept such store
   That all thy body was one door.
Shall I be scourgèd, flouted, boxèd, sold?
   'Tis but to tell the tale is told.
My God, my God, why dost thou part from me?
   Was such a grief as cannot be.   10
Shall I then sing, skipping thy doleful story,
   And side with thy triumphant glory?
Shall thy strokes be my stroking? thorns, my flower?
   Thy rod, my posy? cross, my bower?
But how then shall I imitate thee, and
   Copy thy fair, though bloody hand?
Surely I will revenge me on thy love,

And try who shall victorious prove.
If thou dost give me wealth, I will restore
  All back unto thee by the poor.   20
If thou dost give me honour, men shall see,
  The honour doth belong to thee.
I will not marry; or, if she be mine,
  She and her children shall be thine.
My bosom friend, if he blaspheme thy Name,
  I will tear thence his love and fame.
One half of me being gone, the rest I give
  Unto some chapel, die or live.
As for thy passion—But of that anon,
  When with the other I have done.   30
For thy predestination I'll contrive,
  That three years hence, if I survive,
I'll build a spittle, or mend common ways,
  But mend mine own without delays.
Then I will use the works of thy creation,
  As if I used them but for fashion.
The world and I will quarrel; and the year
  Shall not perceive, that I am here.
My music shall find thee, and ev'ry string
  Shall have his attribute to sing;   40
That all together may accord in thee,
  And prove one God, one harmony.
If thou shalt give me wit, it shall appear,
  If thou hast giv'n it me, 'tis here.
Nay, I will read thy book, and never move
  Till I have found therein thy love,
Thy art of love, which I'll turn back on thee:
  O my dear Saviour, Victory!
Then for thy passion—I will do for that—
Alas, my God, I know not what.   50

The Reprisal

  I have considered it, and find
There is no dealing with thy mighty passion:
For though I die for thee, I am behind;
  My sins deserve the condemnation.

O make me innocent, that I
May give a disentangled state and free:
And yet thy wounds still my attempts defy,
    For by thy death I die for thee.

Ah! was it not enough that thou
By thy eternal glory didst outgo me?   10
Couldst thou not grief's sad conquests me allow,
    But in all vict'ries overthrow me?

Yet by confession will I come
Into thy conquest: though I can do nought
Against thee, in thee I will overcome
    The man, who once against thee fought.

The Agony

Philosophers have measured mountains,
Fathomed the depths of seas, of states, and kings,
Walked with a staff to heav'n, and tracèd fountains:
    But there are two vast, spacious things,
The which to measure it doth more behove:
Yet few there are that sound them; Sin and Love.

Who would know Sin, let him repair
Unto Mount Olivet; there shall he see
A man so wrung with pains, that all his hair,
    His skin, his garments bloody be.   10
Sin is that press and vice, which forceth pain
To hunt his cruel food through ev'ry vein.

Who knows not Love, let him assay
And taste that juice, which on the cross a pike
Did set again abroach; then let him say
    If ever he did taste the like.
Love is that liquor sweet and most divine,
Which my God feels as blood; but I, as wine.

The Sinner

Lord, how I am all ague, when I seek
What I have treasured in my memory!
  Since, if my soul make even with the week,
Each seventh note by right is due to thee.
I find there quarries of piled vanities,
  But shreds of holiness that dare not venture
  To show their face, since cross to thy decrees:
There the circumference earth is, heav'n the centre.
In so much dregs the quintessence is small:
  The spirit and good extract of my heart   10
  Comes to about the many hundred part.
Yet Lord restore thine image, hear my call:
  And though my hard heart scarce to thee can groan,
  Remember that thou once didst write in stone.

Good Friday

  O my chief good,
How shall I measure out thy blood?
How shall I count what thee befell,
  And each grief tell?

  Shall I thy woes
Number according to thy foes?
Or, since one star showed thy first breath,
  Shall all thy death?

  Or shall each leaf,
Which falls in Autumn, score a grief?   10
Or can not leaves, but fruit, be sign
  Of the true vine?

  Then let each hour
Of my whole life one grief devour;
That thy distress through all may run,
  And be my sun.

    Or rather let
My several sins their sorrows get;
That as each beast his cure doth know,
    Each sin may so.   20

Since blood is fittest, Lord, to write
Thy sorrows in, and bloody fight;
My heart hath store, write there, where in
One box doth lie both ink and sin:

That when sin spies so many foes,
Thy whips, thy nails, thy wounds, thy woes,
All come to lodge there, sin may say,
No room for me, and fly away.

Sin being gone, oh fill the place,
And keep possession with thy grace;   30
Lest sin take courage and return,
And all the writings blot or burn.

Redemption

Having been tenant long to a rich Lord,
    Not thriving, I resolvèd to be bold,
    And make a suit unto him, to afford
A new small-rented lease, and cancel th' old.
In heaven at his manor I him sought:
    They told me there, that he was lately gone
    About some land, which he had dearly bought
Long since on earth, to take possession.
I straight returned, and knowing his great birth,
    Sought him accordingly in great resorts;   10
    In cities, theatres, gardens, parks, and courts:
At length I heard a ragged noise and mirth
    Of thieves and murderers: there I him espied,
    Who straight, *Your suit is granted*, said, and died.

Sepulchre

O blessed body! Whither art thou thrown?
No lodging for thee, but a cold hard stone?
So many hearts on earth, and yet not one
       Receive thee?
Sure there is room within our hearts good store;
For they can lodge transgressions by the score:
Thousands of toys dwell there, yet out of door
       They leave thee.

But that which shows them large, shows them unfit.
What ever sin did this pure rock commit,
Which holds thee now? Who hath indicted it
       Of murder?
Where our hard hearts have took up stones to brain thee,
And missing this, most falsely did arraign thee;
Only these stones in quiet entertain thee,
       And order.

And as of old the Law by heav'nly art
Was writ in stone; so thou, which also art
The letter of the word, find'st no fit heart
       To hold thee.
Yet do we still persist as we began,
And so should perish, but that nothing can,
Though it be cold, hard, foul, from loving man
       Withhold thee.

Easter

Rise heart; thy Lord is risen. Sing his praise
       Without delays,
Who takes thee by the hand, that thou likewise
       With him mayst rise:
That, as his death calcinèd thee to dust,
His life may make thee gold, and much more, just.

Awake, my lute, and struggle for thy part
           With all thy art.
The cross taught all wood to resound his name,
           Who bore the same.   10
His stretched sinews taught all strings, what key
Is best to celebrate this most high day.

Consort both heart and lute, and twist a song
           Pleasant and long:
Or, since all music is but three parts vied
           And multiplied,
O let thy blessed Spirit bear a part,
And make up our defects with his sweet art.

  I got me flowers to straw thy way;
  I got me boughs off many a tree: 20
  But thou wast up by break of day,
  And brought'st thy sweets along with thee.

  The sun arising in the East,
  Though he give light, and th' East perfume;
  If they should offer to contest
  With thy arising, they presume.

  Can there be any day but this,
  Though many suns to shine endeavour?
  We count three hundred, but we miss:
  There is but one, and that one ever.   30

Easter-wings

Lord, who createdst man in wealth and store,
 Though foolishly he lost the same,
  Decaying more and more,
   Till he became
    Most poor:
    With thee
    O let me rise
   As larks, harmoniously,
  And sing this day thy victories:
Then shall the fall further the flight in me.   10

My tender age in sorrow did begin:
 And still with sicknesses and shame
  Thou didst so punish sin,
   That I became
    Most thin.
    With thee
   Let me combine
  And feel this day thy victory:
 For, if I imp my wing on thine,
Affliction shall advance the flight in me.   20

H. Baptism (I)

As he that sees a dark and shady grove,
 Stays not, but looks beyond it on the sky;
 So when I view my sins, mine eyes remove
More backward still, and to that water fly,
Which is above the heav'ns, whose spring and vent
 Is in my dear Redeemer's piercèd side.
 O blessed streams! either ye do prevent
And stop our sins from growing thick and wide,
Or else give tears to drown them, as they grow.
 In you Redemption measures all my time,   10
 And spreads the plaster equal to the crime.

You taught the Book of Life my name, that so
What ever future sins should me miscall,
Your first acquaintance might discredit all.

H. Baptism (II)

Since, Lord, to thee
A narrow way and little gate
Is all the passage, on my infancy
Thou didst lay hold, and antedate
My faith in me.

O let me still
Write thee great God, and me a child:
Let me be soft and supple to thy will,
Small to myself, to others mild,
Behither ill.   10

Although by stealth
My flesh get on, yet let her sister
My soul bid nothing, but preserve her wealth:
The growth of flesh is but a blister;
Childhood is health.

Nature

Full of rebellion, I would die,
Or fight, or travel, or deny
That thou hast ought to do with me.
O tame my heart;
It is thy highest art
To captivate strongholds to thee.

If thou shalt let this venom lurk,
And in suggestions fume and work,
My soul will turn to bubbles straight,
And thence by kind   10
Vanish into a wind,
Making thy workmanship deceit.

O smooth my rugged heart, and there
Engrave thy rev'rend Law and fear;
Or make a new one, since the old
               Is sapless grown,
            And a much fitter stone
To hide my dust, than thee to hold.

Sin (I)

Lord, with what care hast thou begirt us round!
  Parents first season us: then schoolmasters
  Deliver us to laws; they send us bound
To rules of reason, holy messengers,
Pulpits and Sundays, sorrow dogging sin,
  Afflictions sorted, anguish of all sizes,
  Fine nets and stratagems to catch us in,
Bibles laid open, millions of surprises,
Blessings beforehand, ties of gratefulness,
  The sound of glory ringing in our ears: 10
  Without, our shame; within, our consciences;
Angels and grace, eternal hopes and fears.
  Yet all these fences and their whole array
  One cunning bosom-sin blows quite away.

Affliction (I)

When first thou didst entice to thee my heart,
            I thought the service brave:
So many joys I writ down for my part,
            Besides what I might have
Out of my stock of natural delights,
Augmented with thy gracious benefits.

I lookèd on thy furniture so fine,
            And made it fine to me:
Thy glorious household-stuff did me entwine,
            And 'tice me unto thee.   10

Such stars I counted mine: both heav'n and earth
Paid me my wages in a world of mirth.

What pleasures could I want, whose King I served,
                    Where joys my fellows were?
Thus argued into hopes, my thoughts reserved
                    No place for grief or fear.
Therefore my sudden soul caught at the place,
And made her youth and fierceness seek thy face.

At first thou gav'st me milk and sweetnesses;
                    I had my wish and way: 20
My days were strawed with flow'rs and happiness;
                    There was no month but May.
But with my years sorrow did twist and grow,
And made a party unawares for woe.

My flesh began unto my soul in pain,
                    Sicknesses cleave my bones;
Consuming agues dwell in ev'ry vein,
                    And tune my breath to groans.
Sorrow was all my soul; I scarce believed,
Till grief did tell me roundly, that I lived.   30

When I got health, thou took'st away my life,
                    And more; for my friends die:
My mirth and edge was lost; a blunted knife
                    Was of more use than I.
Thus thin and lean without a fence or friend,
I was blown through with ev'ry storm and wind.

Whereas my birth and spirit rather took
                    The way that takes the town;
Thou didst betray me to a ling'ring book,
                    And wrap me in a gown.   40
I was entangled in the world of strife,
Before I had the power to change my life.

Yet, for I threatened oft the siege to raise,
                    Not simp'ring all mine age,
Thou often didst with academic praise

                    Melt and dissolve my rage.
I took thy sweetened pill, till I came where
I could not go away, nor persevere.

Yet lest perchance I should too happy be
                    In my unhappiness,
Turning my purge to food, thou throwest me   50
                    Into more sicknesses.
Thus doth thy power cross-bias me, not making
Thine own gift good, yet me from my ways taking.

Now I am here, what thou wilt do with me
                    None of my books will show:
I read, and sigh, and wish I were a tree;
                    For sure then I should grow
To fruit or shade: at least some bird would trust
Her household to me, and I should be just.   60

Yet, though thou troublest me, I must be meek;
                    In weakness must be stout.
Well, I will change the service, and go seek
                    Some other master out.
Ah my dear God! though I am clean forgot,
Let me not love thee, if I love thee not.

Repentance

Lord, I confess my sin is great;
    Great is my sin. Oh! gently treat
With thy quick flow'r, thy momentary bloom;
                    Whose life still pressing
                    Is one undressing,
    A steady aiming at a tomb.

Man's age is two hours' work, or three:
    Each day doth round about us see.
Thus are we to delights: but we are all
                    To sorrows old,   10
                    If life be told
From what life feeleth, Adam's fall.

O let thy height of mercy then
Compassionate short-breathèd men.
Cut me not off for my most foul transgression:
    I do confess
    My foolishness;
My God, accept of my confession.

Sweeten at length this bitter bowl,
Which thou hast poured into my soul;   20
Thy wormwood turn to health, winds to fair weather:
    For if thou stay,
    I and this day,
As we did rise, we die together.

When thou for sin rebukest man,
Forthwith he waxeth woe and wan:
Bitterness fills our bowels; all our hearts
    Pine, and decay,
    And drop away,
And carry with them th' other parts.   30

But thou wilt sin and grief destroy;
That so the broken bones may joy,
And tune together in a well-set song,
    Full of his praises,
    Who dead men raises.
Fractures well cured make us more strong.

Faith

Lord, how couldst thou so much appease
Thy wrath for sin as, when man's sight was dim,
And could see little, to regard his ease,
    And bring by Faith all things to him?

Hungry I was, and had no meat:
I did conceit a most delicious feast;
I had it straight, and did as truly eat,
    As ever did a welcome guest.

There is a rare outlandish root,
Which when I could not get, I thought it here: 10
That apprehension cured so well my foot,
   That I can walk to heav'n well near.

I owèd thousands and much more:
I did believe that I did nothing owe,
And lived accordingly; my creditor
   Believes so too, and lets me go.

Faith makes me anything, or all
That I believe is in the sacred story:
And where sin placeth me in Adam's fall,
   Faith sets me higher in his glory.   20

If I go lower in the book,
What can be lower than the common manger?
Faith puts me there with him, who sweetly took
   Our flesh and frailty, death and danger.

If bliss had lien in art or strength,
None but the wise or strong had gainèd it:
Where now by Faith all arms are of a length;
   One size doth all conditions fit.

A peasant may believe as much
As a great clerk, and reach the highest stature.   30
Thus dost thou make proud knowledge bend and crouch,
   While grace fills up uneven nature.

When creatures had no real light
Inherent in them, thou didst make the sun
Impute a lustre, and allow them bright;
   And in this show, what Christ hath done.

That which before was darkened clean
With bushy groves, pricking the looker's eye,
Vanished away, when Faith did change the scene:
   And then appeared a glorious sky.   40

What though my body run to dust?
Faith cleaves unto it, counting ev'ry grain
With an exact and most particular trust,
    Reserving all for flesh again.

Prayer (I)

Prayer the Church's banquet, angels' age,
    God's breath in man returning to his birth,
    The soul in paraphrase, heart in pilgrimage,
The Christian plummet sounding heav'n and earth;
Engine against th' Almighty, sinners' tower,
    Reversèd thunder, Christ-side-piercing spear,
    The six-days' world transposing in an hour,
A kind of tune, which all things hear and fear;
Softness, and peace, and joy, and love, and bliss,
    Exalted manna, gladness of the best,   10
    Heaven in ordinary, man well dressed,
The milky way, the bird of Paradise,
    Church-bells beyond the stars heard, the soul's blood,
    The land of spices; something understood.

The H. Communion

Not in rich furniture, or fine array,
    Nor in a wedge of gold,
    Thou, who for me wast sold,
To me dost now thyself convey;
For so thou should'st without me still have been,
    Leaving within me sin:

But by the way of nourishment and strength
    Thou creep'st into my breast;
    Making thy way my rest,
And thy small quantities my length;   10
Which spread their forces into every part,
    Meeting sin's force and art.

Yet can these not get over to my soul,
    Leaping the wall that parts
    Our souls and fleshy hearts;
  But as th' outworks, they may control
My rebel-flesh, and carrying thy name,
    Affright both sin and shame.

Only thy grace, which with these elements comes,
    Knoweth the ready way,
    And hath the privy key,   20
  Op'ning the soul's most subtle rooms;
While those to spirits refined, at door attend
    Dispatches from their friend.

Give me my captive soul, or take
  My body also thither.
Another lift like this will make
  Them both to be together.

Before that sin turned flesh to stone,
    And all our lump to leaven;   30
A fervent sigh might well have blown
    Our innocent earth to heaven.

For sure when Adam did not know
    To sin, or sin to smother;
He might to heav'n from Paradise go,
    As from one room t' another.

Thou hast restored us to this ease
    By this thy heav'nly blood;
Which I can go to, when I please,
    And leave th' earth to their food.   40

Antiphon (I)

Cho. Let all the world in ev'ry corner sing,
      My God and King.

  Vers. The heav'ns are not too high,
     His praise may thither fly:
     The earth is not too low,
     His praises there may grow.

Cho. Let all the world in ev'ry corner sing,
      My God and King.

  Vers. The church with psalms must shout,
     No door can keep them out: 10
     But above all, the heart
     Must bear the longest part.

Cho. Let all the world in ev'ry corner sing,
      My God and King.

Love I

Immortal Love, author of this great frame,
  Sprung from that beauty which can never fade;
  How hath man parcelled out thy glorious name,
And thrown it on that dust which thou hast made,
While mortal love doth all the title gain!
  Which siding with invention, they together
  Bear all the sway, possessing heart and brain,
(Thy workmanship) and give thee share in neither.
Wit fancies beauty, beauty raiseth wit:
  The world is theirs; they two play out the game,   10
  Thou standing by: and though thy glorious name
Wrought our deliverance from th'infernal pit,
  Who sings thy praise? only a scarf or glove
  Doth warm our hands, and make them write of love.

II

Immortal Heat, O let thy greater flame
　　Attract the lesser to it: let those fires,
　　Which shall consume the world, first make it tame;
And kindle in our hearts such true desires,
As may consume our lusts, and make thee way.
　　Then shall our hearts pant thee; then shall our brain
　　All her invention on thine Altar lay,
And there in hymns send back thy fire again:
Our eyes shall see thee, which before saw dust;
　　Dust blown by wit, till that they both were blind: 10
　　Thou shalt recover all thy goods in kind,
Who wert disseizèd by usurping lust:
　　All knees shall bow to thee; all wits shall rise,
　　And praise him who did make and mend our eyes.

The Temper (I)

How should I praise thee, Lord! how should my rhymes
　　Gladly engrave thy love in steel,
　　If what my soul doth feel sometimes,
　　　My soul might ever feel!

Although there were some forty heav'ns, or more,
　　Sometimes I peer above them all;
　　Sometimes I hardly reach a score,
　　　Sometimes to hell I fall.

O rack me not to such a vast extent;
　　Those distances belong to thee: 10
　　The world's too little for thy tent,
　　　A grave too big for me.

Wilt thou meet arms with man, that thou dost stretch
　　A crumb of dust from heav'n to hell?
　　Will great God measure with a wretch?
　　　Shall he thy stature spell?

O let me, when thy roof my soul hath hid,
  O let me roost and nestle there:
  Then of a sinner thou art rid,
    And I of hope and fear.   20

Yet take thy way; for sure thy way is best:
  Stretch or contract me, thy poor debtor:
  This is but tuning of my breast,
    To make the music better.

Whether I fly with angels, fall with dust,
  Thy hands made both, and I am there:
  Thy power and love, my love and trust
    Make one place ev'rywhere.

The Temper (II)

It cannot be. Where is that mighty joy,
  Which just now took up all my heart?
  Lord, if thou must needs use thy dart,
Save that, and me; or sin for both destroy.

The grosser world stands to thy word and art;
  But thy diviner world of grace
  Thou suddenly dost raise and race,
And ev'ry day a new Creator art.

O fix thy chair of grace, that all my powers
  May also fix their reverence: 10
  For when thou dost depart from hence,
They grow unruly, and sit in thy bowers.

Scatter, or bind them all to bend to thee:
  Though elements change, and heaven move,
  Let not thy higher Court remove,
But keep a standing Majesty in me.

Jordan (I)

Who says that fictions only and false hair
Become a verse? Is there in truth no beauty,
Is all good structure in a winding stair?
May no lines pass, except they do their duty
  Not to a true, but painted chair?

Is it no verse, except enchanted groves
And sudden arbours shadow coarse-spun lines?
Must purling streams refresh a lover's loves?
Must all be veiled, while he that reads, divines,
  Catching the sense at two removes?   10

Shepherds are honest people; let them sing:
Riddle who list, for me, and pull for prime:
I envy no man's nightingale or spring;
Nor let them punish me with loss of rhyme,
  Who plainly say, *My God, My King*.

Employment (I)

If as a flower doth spread and die,
  Thou wouldst extend me to some good,
Before I were by frost's extremity
         Nipped in the bud;

The sweetness and the praise were thine;
  But the extension and the room,
Which in thy garland I should fill, were mine
         At thy great doom.

For as thou dost impart thy grace,
  The greater shall our glory be.   10
The measure of our joys is in this place,
         The stuff with thee.

Let me not languish then, and spend
   A life as barren to thy praise,
As is the dust, to which that life doth tend,
                But with delays.

All things are busy; only I
   Neither bring honey with the bees,
Nor flowers to make that, nor the husbandry
                To water these.   20

I am no link of thy great chain,
   But all my company is a weed.
Lord place me in thy consort; give one strain
                To my poor reed.

The H. Scriptures. I

Oh Book! infinite sweetness! let my heart
   Suck ev'ry letter, and a honey gain,
   Precious for any grief in any part;
To clear the breast, to mollify all pain.
Thou art all health, health thriving till it make
   A full eternity: thou art a mass
   Of strange delights, where we may wish and take.
Ladies, look here; this is the thankful glass
That mends the looker's eyes: this is the well
   That washes what it shows. Who can endear   10
   Thy praise too much? thou art heav'n's lidger here,
Working against the states of death and hell.
   Thou art joy's handsel: heav'n lies flat in thee,
   Subject to ev'ry mounter's bended knee.

II

Oh that I knew how all thy lights combine,
   And the configurations of their glory!
   Seeing not only how each verse doth shine,
But all the constellations of the story.

This verse marks that, and both do make a motion
 Unto a third, that ten leaves off doth lie:
 Then as dispersèd herbs do watch a potion,
These three make up some Christian's destiny:
Such are thy secrets, which my life makes good,
 And comments on thee: for in ev'rything   10
 Thy words do find me out, and parallels bring,
And in another make me understood.
 Stars are poor books, and oftentimes do miss:
 This book of stars lights to eternal bliss.

Whitsunday

Listen sweet Dove unto my song,
 And spread thy golden wings in me;
 Hatching my tender heart so long,
Till it get wing, and fly away with thee.

Where is that fire which once descended
 On thy Apostles? thou didst then
 Keep open house, richly attended,
Feasting all comers by twelve chosen men.

Such glorious gifts thou didst bestow,
 That th' earth did like a heav'n appear;   10
 The stars were coming down to know
If they might mend their wages, and serve here.

The sun, which once did shine alone,
 Hung down his head, and wished for night,
 When he beheld twelve suns for one
Going about the world, and giving light.

But since those pipes of gold, which brought
 That cordial water to our ground,
 Were cut and martyred by the fault
Of those, who did themselves through their side wound, 20

Thou shutt'st the door and keep'st within;
Scarce a good joy creeps through the chink:
And if the braves of conqu'ring sin
Did not excite thee, we should wholly sink.

Lord, though we change, thou art the same;
The same sweet God of love and light:
Restore this day, for thy great name,
Unto his ancient and miraculous right.

Grace

My stock lies dead, and no increase
Doth my dull husbandry improve:
O let thy graces without cease
      Drop from above!

If still the sun should hide his face,
Thy house would but a dungeon prove,
Thy works night's captives: O let grace
      Drop from above!

The dew doth ev'ry morning fall;
And shall the dew outstrip thy Dove?   10
The dew, for which grass cannot call,
      Drop from above.

Death is still working like a mole,
And digs my grave at each remove:
Let grace work too, and on my soul
      Drop from above.

Sin is still hammering my heart
Unto a hardness void of love:
Let suppling grace, to cross his art,
      Drop from above.   20

O come! for thou dost know the way:
Or if to me thou wilt not move,
Remove me, where I need not say,
      Drop from above.

Praise (I)

To write a verse or two is all the praise,
          That I can raise:
    Mend my estate in any ways,
          Thou shalt have more.

I go to Church; help me to wings, and I
          Will thither fly;
    Or, if I mount unto the sky,
          I will do more.

Man is all weakness; there is no such thing
          As Prince or King: 10
    His arm is short; yet with a sling
          He may do more.

An herb distilled, and drunk, may dwell next door,
          On the same floor,
    To a brave soul: exalt the poor,
          They can do more.

O raise me then! Poor bees, that work all day,
          Sting my delay,
    Who have a work, as well as they,
          And much, much more.   20

Affliction (II)

    Kill me not ev'ry day,
Thou Lord of life; since thy one death for me
Is more than all my deaths can be,
    Though I in broken pay
Die over each hour of Methusalem's stay.

    If all men's tears were let
Into one common sewer, sea, and brine;
  What were they all, compared to thine?
    Wherein if they were set,
They would discolour thy most bloody sweat.   10

Thou art my grief alone,
Thou Lord conceal it not: and as thou art
   All my delight, so all my smart:
        Thy cross took up in one,
By way of imprest, all my future moan.

Mattens

I cannot ope mine eyes,
   But thou art ready there to catch
   My morning-soul and sacrifice:
Then we must needs for that day make a match.

   My God, what is a heart?
   Silver, or gold, or precious stone,
   Or star, or rainbow, or a part
Of all these things, or all of them in one?

   My God, what is a heart,
   That thou shouldst it so eye, and woo,   10
   Pouring upon it all thy art,
As if that thou hadst nothing else to do?

   Indeed man's whole estate
   Amounts (and richly) to serve thee:
   He did not heav'n and earth create,
Yet studies them, not him by whom they be.

   Teach me thy love to know;
   That this new light, which now I see,
   May both the work and workman show:
Then by a sun-beam I will climb to thee.   20

Sin (II)

O that I could a sin once see!
We paint the devil foul, yet he
Hath some good in him, all agree.
Sin is flat opposite to th' Almighty, seeing
It wants the good of *virtue*, and of *being*.

But God more care of us hath had:
If apparitions make us sad,
By sight of sin we should grow mad.
Yet as in sleep we see foul death, and live:
So devils are our sins in perspective.   10

Evensong

Blest be the God of love,
Who gave me eyes, and light, and power this day,
Both to be busy, and to play.
But much more blest be God above,
Who gave me sight alone,
Which to himself he did deny:
For when he sees my ways, I die:
But I have got his son, and he hath none.

What have I brought thee home
For this thy love? have I discharged the debt,   10
Which this day's favour did beget?
I ran; but all I brought, was foam.
Thy diet, care, and cost
Do end in bubbles, balls of wind;
Of wind to thee whom I have crossed,
But balls of wild-fire to my troubled mind.

Yet still thou goest on,
And now with darkness closest weary eyes,
Saying to man, *It doth suffice:*
Henceforth repose; your work is done.

Thus in thy ebony box
Thou dost inclose us, till the day
Put our amendment in our way,
And give new wheels to our disordered clocks.

I muse, which shows more love,
The day or night: that is the gale, this th' harbour;
That is the walk, and this the arbour;
Or that the garden, this the grove.
My God, thou art all love.
Not one poor minute scapes thy breast,   30
But brings a favour from above;
And in this love, more than in bed, I rest.

Church-monuments

While that my soul repairs to her devotion,
Here I intomb my flesh, that it betimes
May take acquaintance of this heap of dust;
To which the blast of death's incessant motion,
Fed with the exhalation of our crimes,
Drives all at last. Therefore I gladly trust
My body to this school, that it may learn
To spell his elements, and find his birth
Written in dusty heraldry and lines;
Which dissolution sure doth best discern,   10
Comparing dust with dust, and earth with earth.
These laugh at jet and marble put for signs,
To sever the good fellowship of dust,
And spoil the meeting. What shall point out them,
When they shall bow, and kneel, and fall down flat
To kiss those heaps, which now they have in trust?
      Dear flesh, while I do pray, learn here thy stem
And true descent; that when thou shalt grow fat,
And wanton in thy cravings, thou mayst know,
That flesh is but the glass, which holds the dust   20
That measures all our time; which also shall
Be crumbled into dust. Mark here below
How tame these ashes are, how free from lust,
That thou mayst fit thyself against thy fall.

Church-music

Sweetest of sweets, I thank you: when displeasure
    Did through my body wound my mind,
You took me thence, and in your house of pleasure
    A dainty lodging me assigned.

Now I in you without a body move,
    Rising and falling with your wings:
We both together sweetly live and love,
    Yet say sometimes, *God help poor Kings*.

Comfort, I'll die; for if you post from me,
    Sure I shall do so, and much more: 10
But if I travel in your company,
    You know the way to heaven's door.

Church-lock and Key

I know it is my sin, which locks thine ears,
    And binds thy hands,
Out-crying my requests, drowning my tears;
Or else the chillness of my faint demands.

But as cold hands are angry with the fire,
    And mend it still;
So I do lay the want of my desire,
Not on my sins, or coldness, but thy will.

Yet hear, O God, only for his blood's sake
    Which pleads for me: 10
For though sins plead too, yet like stones they make
His blood's sweet current much more loud to be.

The Church-floor

Mark you the floor? that square and speckled stone,
        Which looks so firm and strong,
                Is *Patience*:

And th' other black and grave, wherewith each one
        Is checkered all along,
                Humility:

The gentle rising, which on either hand
        Leads to the Choir above,
                Is *Confidence*:

But the sweet cement, which in one sure band   10
        Ties the whole frame, is *Love*
                And *Charity*.

        Hither sometimes Sin steals, and stains
        The marble's neat and curious veins:
But all is cleansèd when the marble weeps.
        Sometimes Death, puffing at the door,
        Blows all the dust about the floor:
But while he thinks to spoil the room, he sweeps.
        Blest be the *Architect*, whose art
        Could build so strong in a weak heart.   20

The Windows

Lord, how can man preach thy eternal word?
        He is a brittle crazy glass:
Yet in thy temple thou dost him afford
        This glorious and transcendent place,
        To be a window, through thy grace.

But when thou dost anneal in glass thy story,
        Making thy life to shine within

The holy preacher's; then the light and glory
   More rev'rend grows, and more doth win:
   Which else shows wat'rish, bleak, and thin.   10

Doctrine and life, colours and light, in one
   When they combine and mingle, bring
A strong regard and awe: but speech alone
   Doth vanish like a flaring thing,
   And in the ear, not conscience ring.

Trinity Sunday

Lord, who hast formed me out of mud,
  And hast redeemed me through thy blood,
  And sanctified me to do good;

Purge all my sins done heretofore:
  For I confess my heavy score,
  And I will strive to sin no more.

Enrich my heart, mouth, hands in me,
  With faith, with hope, with charity;
  That I may run, rise, rest with thee.

Content

Peace mutt'ring thoughts, and do not grudge to keep
   Within the walls of your own breast:
Who cannot on his own bed sweetly sleep,
   Can on another's hardly rest.

Gad not abroad at ev'ry quest and call
   Of an untrainèd hope or passion.
To court each place or fortune that doth fall,
   Is wantonness in contemplation.

Mark how the fire in flints doth quiet lie,
   Content and warm t' itself alone: 10
But when it would appear to other's eye,
   Without a knock it never shone.

Give me the pliant mind, whose gentle measure
   Complies and suits with all estates;
Which can let loose to a crown, and yet with pleasure
   Take up within a cloister's gates.

This soul doth span the world, and hang content
   From either pole unto the centre:
Where in each room of the well-furnished tent
   He lies warm, and without adventure.   20

The brags of life are but a nine-days' wonder;
   And after death the fumes that spring
From private bodies make as big a thunder,
   As those which rise from a huge King.

Only thy Chronicle is lost; and yet
   Better by worms be all once spent,
Than to have hellish moths still gnaw and fret
   Thy name in books, which may not rent:

When all thy deeds, whose brunt thou feel'st alone,
   Are chawed by others' pens and tongue;   30
And as their wit is, their digestion,
   Thy nourished fame is weak or strong.

Then cease discoursing soul, till thine own ground,
   Do not thyself or friends importune.
He that by seeking hath himself once found,
   Hath ever found a happy fortune.

The Quiddity

My God, a verse is not a crown,
No point of honour, or gay suit,
No hawk, or banquet, or renown,
Nor a good sword, nor yet a lute:

It cannot vault, or dance, or play;
It never was in France or Spain, *EP*
Nor can it entertain the day
With my great stable or demesne:

It is no office, art, or news,
Nor the Exchange, or busy Hall;   10
But it is that which while I use
I am with thee, and *most take all*.

Humility

I saw the Virtues sitting hand in hand
In sev'ral ranks upon an azure throne,
Where all the beasts and fowl by their command
Presented tokens of submission.
Humility, who sat the lowest there
               To execute their call,
When by the beasts the presents tendered were,
               Gave them about to all.

The angry Lion did present his paw,
Which by consent was giv'n to Mansuetude.   10
The fearful Hare her ears, which by their law
Humility did reach to Fortitude.
The jealous Turkey brought his coral-chain;
               That went to Temperance.
On Justice was bestowed the Fox's brain,
               Killed in the way by chance.

At length the Crow bringing the Peacock's plume,
(For he would not) as they beheld the grace
Of that brave gift, each one began to fume,
And challenge it, as proper to his place,   20
Till they fell out: which when the beasts espied,
               They leapt upon the throne;
And if the fox had lived to rule their side,
               They had deposed each one.

Humility, who held the plume, at this
Did weep so fast, that the tears trickling down
Spoiled all the train: then saying, *Here it is*
For which ye wrangle, made them turn their frown
Against the beasts: so jointly bandying,
              They drive them soon away;   30
And then amerced them, double gifts to bring
              At the next Session-day.

Frailty

Lord, in my silence how do I despise
          What upon trust
Is stylèd *honour*, *riches*, or *fair eyes*;
          But is *fair dust*!
    I surname them *gilded clay*,
      Dear earth, fine grass or *hay*;
In all I think my foot doth ever tread
          Upon their head.

But when I view abroad both Regiments;
          The world's, and thine: 10
Thine clad with simpleness, and sad events;
          The other fine,
    Full of glory and gay weeds,
      Brave language, braver deeds:
That which was dust before, doth quickly rise,
          And prick mine eyes.

O brook not this, lest if what even now
          My foot did tread,
Affront those joys; wherewith thou didst endow
          And long since wed   20
    My poor soul, ev'n sick of love:
      It may a Babel prove
Commodious to conquer heav'n and thee
          Planted in me.

Constancy

Who is the honest man?
He that doth still and strongly good pursue,
To God, his neighbour, and himself most true:
    Whom neither force nor fawning can
Unpin, or wrench from giving all their due.

    Whose honesty is not
So loose or easy, that a ruffling wind
Can blow away, or glittering look it blind:
    Who rides his sure and even trot,
While the world now rides by, now lags behind.   10

    Who, when great trials come,
Nor seeks, nor shuns them; but doth calmly stay,
Till he the thing and the example weigh:
    All being brought into a sum,
What place or person calls for, he doth pay.

    Whom none can work or woo
To use in anything a trick or sleight;
For above all things he abhors deceit:
    His words and works and fashion too
All of a piece, and all are clear and straight.   20

    Who never melts or thaws
At close tentations: when the day is done,
His goodness sets not, but in dark can run:
    The sun to others writeth laws,
And is their virtue; Virtue is his Sun.

    Who, when he is to treat
With sick folks, women, those whom passions sway,
Allows for that, and keeps his constant way:
    Whom others' faults do not defeat;
But though men fail him, yet his part doth play.   30

    Whom nothing can procure,
When the wide world runs bias from his will,
To writhe his limbs, and share, not mend the ill.
    This is the mark-man, safe and sure,
Who still is right, and prays to be so still.

Affliction (III)

My heart did heave, and there came forth, *O God!*
By that I knew that thou wast in the grief,
To guide and govern it to my relief,
      Making a scepter of the rod:
         Hadst thou not had thy part,
Sure the unruly sigh had broke my heart.

But since thy breath gave me both life and shape,
Thou know'st my tallies; and when there's assigned
So much breath to a sigh, what's then behind?
      Or if some years with it escape,   10
         The sigh then only is
A gale to bring me sooner to my bliss.

Thy life on earth was grief, and thou art still
Constant unto it, making it to be
A point of honour, now to grieve in me,
      And in thy members suffer ill.
         They who lament one cross,
Thou dying daily, praise thee to thy loss.

The Star

    Bright spark, shot from a brighter place,
      Where beams surround my Saviour's face,
        Canst thou be anywhere
        So well as there?

    Yet, if thou wilt from thence depart,
      Take a bad lodging in my heart;
        For thou canst make a debtor,
        And make it better.

    First, with thy fire-work burn to dust
      Folly, and worse than folly, lust: 10
        Then with thy light refine,
        And make it shine:

So disengaged from sin and sickness,
  Touch it with thy celestial quickness,
    That it may hang and move
      After thy love.

Then with our trinity of light,
  Motion, and heat, let's take our flight
    Unto the place where thou
      Before didst bow.   20

Get me a standing there, and place
  Among the beams, which crown the face
    Of him, who died to part
      Sin and my heart:

That so among the rest I may
  Glitter, and curl, and wind as they:
    That winding is their fashion
      Of adoration.

Sure thou wilt joy, by gaining me
  To fly home like a laden bee   30
    Unto that hive of beams
      And garland-streams.

Sunday

    O day most calm, most bright,
The fruit of this, the next world's bud,
Th' endorsement of supreme delight,
Writ by a friend, and with his blood;
The couch of time; care's balm and bay:
The week were dark, but for thy light:
    Thy torch doth show the way.

    The other days and thou
Make up one man; whose face thou art,
Knocking at heaven with thy brow: 10
The worky-days are the back-part;

The burden of the week lies there,
Making the whole to stoop and bow,
        Till thy release appear.

        Man had straight forward gone
To endless death: but thou dost pull
And turn us round to look on one,
Whom, if we were not very dull,
We could not choose but look on still;
Since there is no place so alone,   20
        The which he doth not fill.

        Sundays the pillars are,
On which heav'n's palace archèd lies:
The other days fill up the spare
And hollow room with vanities.
They are the fruitful beds and borders
In God's rich garden: that is bare,
        Which parts their ranks and orders.

        The Sundays of man's life,
Threaded together on time's string,   30
Make bracelets to adorn the wife
Of the eternal glorious King.
On Sunday heaven's gate stands ope;
Blessings are plentiful and rife,
        More plentiful than hope.

        This day my Saviour rose,
And did inclose this light for his:
That, as each beast his manger knows,
Man might not of his fodder miss.
Christ hath took in this piece of ground,   40
And made a garden there for those
        Who want herbs for their wound.

        The rest of our Creation
Our great Redeemer did remove
With the same shake, which at his passion
Did th' earth and all things with it move.
As Sampson bore the doors away,
Christ's hands, though nailed, wrought our salvation,
        And did unhinge that day.

The brightness of that day   50
We sullied by our foul offence:
Wherefore that robe we cast away,
Having a new at his expense,
Whose drops of blood paid the full price,
That was required to make us gay,
    And fit for Paradise.

Thou art a day of mirth:
And where the week-days trail on ground,
Thy flight is higher, as thy birth.
O let me take thee at the bound,   60
Leaping with thee from sev'n to sev'n,
Till that we both, being tossed from earth,
    Fly hand in hand to heav'n!

Avarice

Money, thou bane of bliss, and source of woe,
    Whence com'st thou, that thou art so fresh and fine?
    I know thy parentage is base and low:
Man found thee poor and dirty in a mine.
Surely thou didst so little contribute
    To this great kingdom, which thou now hast got,
    That he was fain, when thou wert destitute,
To dig thee out of thy dark cave and grot:
Then forcing thee by fire he made thee bright:
    Nay, thou hast got the face of man; for we   10
    Have with our stamp and seal transferred our right:
Thou art the man, and man but dross to thee.
    Man calleth thee his wealth, who made thee rich;
    And while he digs out thee, falls in the ditch.

Ana- $\left\{ \begin{array}{c} \text{MARY} \\ \text{ARMY} \end{array} \right\}$ *gram*

How well her name an *Army* doth present,
In whom the *Lord of Hosts* did pitch his tent!

To All Angels and Saints

Oh glorious spirits, who after all your bands
See the smooth face of God without a frown
           Or strict commands;
Where ev'ry one is king, and hath his crown,
If not upon his head, yet in his hands:

Not out of envy or maliciousness
Do I forbear to crave your special aid:
           I would address
My vows to thee most gladly, Blessed Maid,
And Mother of my God, in my distress.   10

Thou art the holy mine, whence came the gold,
The great restorative for all decay
           In young and old;
Thou art the cabinet where the jewel lay:
Chiefly to thee would I my soul unfold:

But now, alas, I dare not; for our King,
Whom we do all jointly adore and praise,
           Bids no such thing:
And where his pleasure no injunction lays,
('Tis your own case) ye never move a wing.   20

All worship is prerogative, and a flower
Of his rich crown, from whom lies no appeal
           At the last hour:
Therefore we dare not from his garland steal,
To make a posy for inferior power.

Although then others court you, if ye know
What's done on earth, we shall not fare the worse,
           Who do not so;
Since we are ever ready to disburse,
If anyone our Master's hand can show.   30

Employment (II)

He that is weary, let him sit.
        My soul would stir
And trade in courtesies and wit,
        Quitting the fur
To cold complexions needing it.

Man is no star, but a quick coal
        Of mortal fire:
Who blows it not, nor doth control
        A faint desire,
Lets his own ashes choke his soul.   10

When th' elements did for place contest
        With him, whose will
Ordained the highest to be best,
        The earth sat still,
And by the others is oppressed.

Life is a business, not good cheer;
        Ever in wars.
The sun still shineth there or here,
        Whereas the stars
Watch an advantage to appear.   20

Oh that I were an orange-tree,
        That busy plant!
Then should I ever laden be,
        And never want
Some fruit for him that dressèd me.

But we are still too young or old;
        The Man is gone,
Before we do our wars unfold:
        So we freeze on,
Until the grave increase our cold.   30

Denial

When my devotions could not pierce
                    Thy silent ears;
Then was my heart broken, as was my verse:
          My breast was full of fears
                              And disorder:

My bent thoughts, like a brittle bow,
                    Did fly asunder:
Each took his way; some would to pleasures go,
          Some to the wars and thunder
                              Of alarms.   10

As good go anywhere, they say,
                    As to benumb
Both knees and heart, in crying night and day,
          Come, come, my God, O come,
                              But no hearing.

O that thou shouldst give dust a tongue
                    To cry to thee,
And then not hear it crying! all day long
          My heart was in my knee,
                              But no hearing.   20

Therefore my soul lay out of sight,
                    Untuned, unstrung:
My feeble spirit, unable to look right,
          Like a nipped blossom, hung
                              Discontented.

O cheer and tune my heartless breast,
                    Defer no time;
That so thy favours granting my request,
          They and my mind may chime,
                              And mend my rhyme.   30

Christmas

All after pleasures as I rid one day,
  My horse and I, both tired, body and mind,
  With full cry of affections, quite astray,
I took up in the next inn I could find.
There when I came, whom found I but my dear,
  My dearest Lord, expecting till the grief
  Of pleasures brought me to him, ready there
To be all passengers' most sweet relief?
O Thou, whose glorious, yet contracted light,
  Wrapped in night's mantle, stole into a manger;
  Since my dark soul and brutish is thy right,   10
To man of all beasts be not thou a stranger:
  Furnish and deck my soul, that thou mayst have
  A better lodging than a rack or grave.

The shepherds sing; and shall I silent be?
        My God, no hymn for thee?
My soul's a shepherd too; a flock it feeds
        Of thoughts, and words, and deeds.
The pasture is thy word: the streams, thy grace
        Enriching all the place.   20
Shepherd and flock shall sing, and all my powers
        Out-sing the daylight hours.
Then we will chide the sun for letting night
        Take up his place and right:
We sing one common Lord; wherefore he should
        Himself the candle hold.
I will go searching, till I find a sun
        Shall stay, till we have done;
A willing shiner, that shall shine as gladly,
        As frost-nipped suns look sadly.
Then we will sing, and shine all our own day,   30
        And one another pay:
His beams shall cheer my breast, and both so twine,
Till ev'n his beams sing, and my music shine.

Ungratefulness

Lord, with what bounty and rare clemency
　　　　Hast thou redeemed us from the grave!
　　　　　　If thou hadst let us run,
　　　　　Gladly had man adored the sun,
　　　　　　　And thought his god most brave;
Where now we shall be better gods than he.

Thou hast but two rare cabinets full of treasure,
　　　　The *Trinity*, and *Incarnation*:
　　　　　　Thou hast unlocked them both,
　　　　　And made them jewels to betroth　　　　10
　　　　　　The work of thy creation
Unto thyself in everlasting pleasure.

The statelier cabinet is the *Trinity*,
　　　　Whose sparkling light access denies:
　　　　　　Therefore thou dost not show
　　　　　This fully to us, till death blow
　　　　　　The dust into our eyes:
For by that powder thou wilt make us see.

But all thy sweets are packed up in the other;
　　　　Thy mercies thither flock and flow:　　　20
　　　　　　That as the first affrights,
　　　　　This may allure us with delights;
　　　　　　Because this box we know;
For we have all of us just such another.

But man is close, reserved, and dark to thee:
　　　　When thou demandest but a heart,
　　　　　　He cavils instantly.
　　　　　In his poor cabinet of bone
　　　　　　Sins have their box apart,
Defrauding thee, who gavest two for one.　　　30

Sighs and Groans

O do not use me
After my sins! look not on my desert,
But on thy glory! then thou wilt reform
And not refuse me: for thou only art
The mighty God, but I a silly worm;
O do not bruise me!

O do not urge me!
For what account can thy ill steward make?
I have abused thy stock, destroyed thy woods,
Sucked all thy magazines: my head did ache,   10
Till it found out how to consume thy goods:
O do not scourge me!

O do not blind me!
I have deserved that an Egyptian night
Should thicken all my powers; because my lust
Hath still sewed fig-leaves to exclude thy light:
But I am frailty, and already dust;
O do not grind me!

O do not fill me
With the turned vial of thy bitter wrath!   20
For thou hast other vessels full of blood,
A part whereof my Saviour emptied hath,
Ev'n unto death: since he died for my good,
O do not kill me!

But O reprieve me!
For thou hast life and death at thy command;
Thou art both *Judge* and *Saviour, feast* and *rod,*
Cordial and *Corrosive*: put not thy hand
Into the bitter box; but O my God,
My God, relieve me!   30

The World

Love built a stately house; where Fortune came,
And spinning fancies, she was heard to say,
That her fine cobwebs did support the frame,
Whereas they were supported by the same:
But Wisdom quickly swept them all away.

Then Pleasure came, who, liking not the fashion,
Began to make Balconies, Terraces,
Till she had weakened all by alteration:
But rev'rend laws, and many a proclamation
Reformèd all at length with menaces.   10

Then entered Sin, and with that Sycamore,
Whose leaves first sheltered man from drought and dew,
Working and winding slyly evermore,
The inward walls and sommers cleft and tore:
But Grace shored these, and cut that as it grew.

Then Sin combined with Death in a firm band
To raze the building to the very floor:
Which they effected, none could them withstand.
But Love and Grace took Glory by the hand,
And built a braver palace than before.   20

Coloss. 3. 3
Our life is hid with Christ in God

My words and thoughts do both express this notion,
That *Life* hath with the sun a double motion.
The first *Is* straight, and our diurnal friend,
The other *Hid* and doth obliquely bend.
One life is wrapped *In* flesh, and tends to earth:
The other winds towards *Him*, whose happy birth
Taught me to live here so, *That* still one eye
Should aim and shoot at that which *Is* on high:
Quitting with daily labour all *My* pleasure,
To gain at harvest an eternal *Treasure*.   10

Vanity (I)

The fleet astronomer can bore,
And thread the spheres with his quick-piercing mind:
He views their stations, walks from door to door,
      Surveys, as if he had designed
To make a purchase there: he sees their dances,
      And knoweth long before
Both their full-eyed aspects, and secret glances.

The nimble diver with his side
Cuts through the working waves, that he may fetch
His dearly-earnèd pearl, which God did hide   10
      On purpose from the vent'rous wretch:
That he might save his life, and also hers,
      Who with excessive pride
Her own destruction and his danger wears.

The subtle chymick can devest
And strip the creature naked, till he find
The callow principles within their nest:
      There he imparts to them his mind,
Admitted to their bed-chamber, before
      They appear trim and dressed   20
To ordinary suitors at the door.

What hath not man sought out and found,
But his dear God? who yet his glorious law
Embosoms in us, mellowing the ground
      With showers and frosts, with love and awe,
So that we need not say, Where's this command?
      Poor man, thou searchest round
To find out *death*, but missest *life* at hand.

Lent

Welcome dear feast of Lent: who loves not thee,
He loves not temperance, or authority,
      But is composed of passion.
The Scriptures bid us *fast*; the Church says, *now*:

Give to thy Mother, what thou wouldst allow
        To ev'ry Corporation.

The humble soul composed of love and fear
Begins at home, and lays the burden there,
        When doctrines disagree.
He says, in things which use hath justly got,   10
I am a scandal to the Church, and not
        The Church is so to me.

True Christians should be glad of an occasion
To use their temperance, seeking no evasion,
        When good is seasonable;
Unless authority, which should increase
The obligation in us, make it less,
        And power itself disable.

Besides the cleanness of sweet abstinence,
Quick thoughts and motions at a small expense,   20
        A face not fearing light:
Whereas in fullness there are sluttish fumes,
Sour exhalations, and dishonest rheums,
        Revenging the delight.

Then those same pendant profits, which the spring
And Easter intimate, enlarge the thing,
        And goodness of the deed.
Neither ought other men's abuse of Lent
Spoil the good use; lest by that argument
        We forfeit all our Creed.   30

It's true, we cannot reach Christ's fortieth day;
Yet to go part of that religious way,
        Is better than to rest:
We cannot reach our Saviour's purity;
Yet are we bid, *Be holy ev'n as he.*
        In both let's do our best.

Who goeth in the way which Christ hath gone,
Is much more sure to meet with him, than one
        That travelleth by-ways:

Perhaps my God, though he be far before,   40
May turn, and take me by the hand, and more
          May strengthen my decays.

Yet Lord instruct us to improve our fast
By starving sin and taking such repast
          As may our faults control:
That ev'ry man may revel at his door,
Not in his parlour; banqueting the poor,
          And among those his soul.

Virtue

Sweet day, so cool, so calm, so bright,
The bridal of the earth and sky:
The dew shall weep thy fall tonight;
          For thou must die.

Sweet rose, whose hue angry and brave
Bids the rash gazer wipe his eye:
Thy root is ever in its grave,
          And thou must die.

Sweet spring, full of sweet days and roses,
A box where sweets compacted lie;   10
My music shows ye have your closes,
          And all must die.

Only a sweet and virtuous soul,
Like seasoned timber, never gives;
But though the whole world turn to coal,
          Then chiefly lives.

The Pearl. Matth. 13. 45

I know the ways of Learning; both the head
And pipes that feed the press, and make it run;
What reason hath from nature borrowèd,
Or of itself, like a good huswife, spun

In laws and policy; what the stars conspire,
What willing nature speaks, what forced by fire;
Both th' old discoveries, and the new-found seas,
The stock and surplus, cause and history:
All these stand open, or I have the keys:
         Yet I love thee.   10

I know the ways of Honour, what maintains
The quick returns of courtesy and wit:
In vies of favours whether party gains,
When glory swells the heart, and mouldeth it
To all expressions both of hand and eye,
Which on the world a true-love-knot may tie,
And bear the bundle, wheresoe'er it goes:
How many drams of spirit there must be
To sell my life unto my friends or foes:
         Yet I love thee.   20

I know the ways of Pleasure, the sweet strains,
The lullings and the relishes of it;
The propositions of hot blood and brains;
What mirth and music mean; what love and wit
Have done these twenty hundred years, and more:
I know the projects of unbridled store:
My stuff is flesh, not brass; my senses live,
And grumble oft, that they have more in me
Than he that curbs them, being but one to five:
         Yet I love thee.   30

I know all these, and have them in my hand:
Therefore not sealèd, but with open eyes
I fly to thee, and fully understand
Both the main sale, and the commodities;
And at what rate and price I have thy love;
With all the circumstances that may move:
Yet through these labyrinths, not my grovelling wit,
But thy silk twist let down from heav'n to me,
Did both conduct and teach me, how by it
         To climb to thee.   40

Affliction (IV)

Broken in pieces all asunder,
      Lord, hunt me not,
      A thing forgot,
Once a poor creature, now a wonder,
      A wonder tortured in the space
      Betwixt this world and that of grace.

My thoughts are all a case of knives,
      Wounding my heart
      With scattered smart,
As wat'ring pots give flowers their lives.
      Nothing their fury can control,   10
      While they do wound and pink my soul.

All my attendants are at strife,
      Quitting their place
      Unto my face:
Nothing performs the task of life:
      The elements are let loose to fight,
      And while I live, try out their right.

Oh help, my God! let not their plot
      Kill them and me,   20
      And also thee,
Who art my life: dissolve the knot,
      As the sun scatters by his light
      All the rebellions of the night.

Then shall those powers, which work for grief,
      Enter thy pay,
      And day by day
Labour thy praise, and my relief;
      With care and courage building me,
      Till I reach heav'n, and much more, thee.   30

Man

My God, I heard this day,
That none doth build a stately habitation,
    But he that means to dwell therein.
    What house more stately hath there been,
Or can be, than is Man? to whose creation
    All things are in decay.

    For Man is ev'ry thing,
And more: he is a tree, yet bears more fruit;
    A beast, yet is, or should be more:
    Reason and speech we only bring.   10
Parrots may thank us, if they are not mute,
    They go upon the score.

    Man is all symmetry,
Full of proportions, one limb to another,
    And all to all the world besides:
    Each part may call the furthest, brother:
For head with foot hath private amity,
    And both with moons and tides.

    Nothing hath got so far,
But Man hath caught and kept it, as his prey.   20
    His eyes dismount the highest star:
    He is in little all the sphere.
Herbs gladly cure our flesh; because that they
    Find their acquaintance there.

    For us the winds do blow,
The earth doth rest, heav'n move, and fountains flow.
    Nothing we see, but means our good,
    As our delight, or as our treasure:
The whole is, either our cupboard of food,
    Or cabinet of pleasure.   30

    The stars have us to bed;
Night draws the curtain, which the sun withdraws;
    Music and light attend our head.

All things unto our flesh are kind
In their descent and being; to our mind
  In their ascent and cause.

  Each thing is full of duty:
Waters united are our navigation;
  Distinguishèd, our habitation;
  Below, our drink; above, our meat;
Both are our cleanliness. Hath one such beauty?   40
  Then how are all things neat!

  More servants wait on Man,
Than he'll take notice of: in ev'ry path
  He treads down that which doth befriend him,
  When sickness makes him pale and wan.
Oh mighty love! Man is one world, and hath
  Another to attend him.

  Since then, my God, thou hast
So brave a palace built; O dwell in it,
  That it may dwell with thee at last!   50
  Till then, afford us so much wit,
That, as the world serves us, we may serve thee,
  And both thy servants be.

Antiphon (II)

Chor.   Praisèd be the God of love,
    Men.   Here below,
    Angels.   And here above:
Cho.   Who hath dealt his mercies so,
    Ang.   To his friend,
    Men.   And to his foe;

Cho.   That both grace and glory tend
    Ang.   Us of old,
    Men.   And us in th' end.
Cho.   The great shepherd of the fold   10
    Ang.   Us did make,
    Men.   For us was sold.

Cho.   He our foes in pieces brake;
      Ang.   Him we touch;
      Men.   And him we take.
Cho.   Wherefore since that he is such,
      Ang.   We adore,
      Men.   And we do crouch.

Cho.   Lord, thy praises should be more.
      Men.   We have none,   20
      Ang.   And we no store.
Cho.   Praisèd be the God alone,
      Who hath made of two folds one.

Unkindness

Lord, make me coy and tender to offend:
In friendship, first I think, if that agree,
      Which I intend,
    Unto my friend's intent and end.
I would not use a friend, as I use Thee.

If any touch my friend, or his good name,
It is my honour and my love to free
      His blasted fame
    From the least spot or thought of blame.
I could not use a friend, as I use Thee.   10

My friend may spit upon my curious floor:
Would he have gold? I lend it instantly;
      But let the poor,
    And thou within them, starve at door.
I cannot use a friend, as I use Thee.

When that my friend pretendeth to a place,
I quit my interest, and leave it free:
      But when thy grace
    Sues for my heart, I thee displace,
Nor would I use a friend, as I use Thee.   20

Yet can a friend what thou hast done fulfil?
O write in brass, *My God upon a tree*
                    His blood did spill
            Only to purchase my good-will.
Yet use I not my foes, as I use thee.

Life

I made a posy, while the day ran by:
Here will I smell my remnant out and tie
                    My life within this band.
But Time did beckon to the flowers, and they
By noon most cunningly did steal away,
                    And withered in my hand.

My hand was next to them, and then my heart:
I took, without more thinking, in good part
                    Time's gentle admonition:
Who did so sweetly death's sad taste convey,   10
Making my mind to smell my fatal day;
                    Yet sug'ring the suspicion.

Farewell dear flowers, sweetly your time ye spent,
Fit, while ye lived, for smell or ornament,
                    And after death for cures.
I follow straight without complaints or grief,
Since if my scent be good, I care not if
                    It be as short as yours.

Submission

But that thou art my wisdom, Lord,
        And both mine eyes are thine,
My mind would be extremely stirred
        For missing my design.

Were it not better to bestow
    Some place and power on me?
Then should thy praises with me grow,
    And share in my degree.

But when I thus dispute and grieve,
    I do resume my sight,   10
And pilf'ring what I once did give,
    Disseize thee of thy right.

How know I, if thou shouldst me raise,
    That I should then raise thee?
Perhaps great places and thy praise
    Do not so well agree.

Wherefore unto my gift I stand;
    I will no more advise:
Only do thou lend me a hand,
    Since thou hast both mine eyes.   20

Justice (I)

    I cannot skill of these thy ways.
Lord, thou didst make me, yet thou woundest me;
Lord, thou dost wound me, yet thou dost relieve me:
Lord, thou relievest, yet I die by thee:
Lord, thou dost kill me, yet thou dost reprieve me.
    But when I mark my life and praise,
    Thy justice me most fitly pays:
For, I do praise thee, yet I praise thee not:
My prayers mean thee, yet my prayers stray:
I would do well, yet sin the hand hath got: 10
My soul doth love thee, yet it loves delay.
    I cannot skill of these my ways.

Charms and Knots

Who read a chapter when they rise,
Shall ne'er be troubled with ill eyes.

A poor man's rod, when thou dost ride,
Is both a weapon and a guide.

Who shuts his hand, hath lost his gold:
Who opens it, hath it twice told.

Who goes to bed and does not pray,
Maketh two nights to ev'ry day.

Who by aspersions throw a stone
At th' head of others, hit their own. 10

Who looks on ground with humble eyes,
Finds himself there, and seeks to rise.

When th' hair is sweet through pride or lust,
The powder doth forget the dust.

Take one from ten, and what remains?
Ten still, if sermons go for gains.

In shallow waters heav'n doth show;
But who drinks on, to hell may go.

Affliction (V)

My God, I read this day,
That planted Paradise was not so firm,
As was and is thy floating Ark; whose stay
And anchor thou art only, to confirm
And strengthen it in ev'ry age,
When waves do rise, and tempests rage.

At first we lived in pleasure;
Thine own delights thou didst to us impart:
When we grew wanton, thou didst use displeasure
To make us thine: yet that we might not part,   10
    As we at first did board with thee,
    Now thou wouldst taste our misery.

There is but joy and grief;
If either will convert us, we are thine:
Some angels used the first; if our relief
Take up the second, then thy double line
    And sev'ral baits in either kind
    Furnish thy table to thy mind.

Affliction then is ours;
We are the trees, whom shaking fastens more,   20
While blust'ring winds destroy the wanton bowers,
And ruffle all their curious knots and store.
    My God, so temper joy and woe,
    That thy bright beams may tame thy bow.

Mortification

How soon doth man decay!
When clothes are taken from a chest of sweets
    To swaddle infants, whose young breath
    Scarce knows the way;
    Those clouts are little winding sheets,
Which do consign and send them unto death.

When boys go first to bed,
They step into their voluntary graves,
    Sleep binds them fast; only their breath
    Makes them not dead: 10
    Successive nights, like rolling waves,
Convey them quickly, who are bound for death.

When youth is frank and free,
And calls for music, while his veins do swell,
All day exchanging mirth and breath
In company;
That music summons to the knell,
Which shall befriend him at the hour of death.

When man grows staid and wise,
Getting a house and home, where he may move   20
Within the circle of his breath,
Schooling his eyes;
That dumb inclosure maketh love
Unto the coffin, that attends his death.

When age grows low and weak,
Marking his grave, and thawing ev'ry year,
Till all do melt, and drown his breath
When he would speak;
A chair or litter shows the bier,
Which shall convey him to the house of death.   30

Man, ere he is aware,
Hath put together a solemnity,
And dressed his hearse, while he has breath
As yet to spare:
Yet Lord, instruct us so to die,
That all these dyings may be life in death.

Decay

Sweet were the days, when thou didst lodge with Lot,
Struggle with Jacob, sit with Gideon,
Advise with Abraham, when thy power could not
Encounter Moses' strong complaints and moan:
Thy words were then, *Let me alone*.

One might have sought and found thee presently
At some fair oak, or bush, or cave, or well:
Is my God this way? No, they would reply:

He is to Sinai gone, as we heard tell:
      List, ye may hear great Aaron's bell.   10

But now thou dost thyself immure and close
In some one corner of a feeble heart:
Where yet both Sin and Satan, thy old foes,
Do pinch and straiten thee, and use much art
      To gain thy thirds and little part.

I see the world grows old, whenas the heat
Of thy great love, once spread, as in an urn
Doth closet up itself, and still retreat,
Cold Sin still forcing it, till it return,
      And calling *Justice*, all things burn.   20

Misery

    Lord, let the angels praise thy name.
Man is a foolish thing, a foolish thing,
    Folly and Sin play all his game.
His house still burns, and yet he still doth sing,
      Man is but grass,
      He knows it, fill the glass.

    How canst thou brook his foolishness?
Why, he'll not lose a cup of drink for thee:
    Bid him but temper his excess;
Not he: he knows where he can better be,   10
      As he will swear,
      Than to serve thee in fear.

    What strange pollutions doth he wed,
And make his own? as if none knew but he.
    No man shall beat into his head,
That thou within his curtains drawn canst see:
      They are of cloth,
      Where never yet came moth.

The best of men, turn but thy hand
For one poor minute, stumble at a pin: 20
  They would not have their actions scanned,
Nor any sorrow tell them that they sin,
      Though it be small,
      And measure not their fall.

    They quarrel thee, and would give over
The bargain made to serve thee: but thy love
    Holds them unto it, and doth cover
Their follies with the wing of thy mild Dove,
      Not suff'ring those
      Who would, to be thy foes.   30

    My God, Man cannot praise thy name:
Thou art all brightness, perfect purity;
    The sun holds down his head for shame,
Dead with eclipses, when we speak of thee:
      How shall infection
      Presume on thy perfection?

    As dirty hands foul all they touch,
And those things most, which are most pure and fine:
    So our clay hearts, ev'n when we crouch
To sing thy praises, make them less divine.   40
      Yet either this,
      Or none, thy portion is.

    Man cannot serve thee; let him go,
And serve the swine: there, there is his delight:
    He doth not like this virtue, no;
Give him his dirt to wallow in all night:
      These Preachers make
      His head to shoot and ache.

    Oh foolish man! where are thine eyes?
How hast thou lost them in a crowd of cares?
    Thou pull'st the rug, and wilt not rise,   50
No, not to purchase the whole pack of stars:
      There let them shine,
      Thou must go sleep, or dine.

The bird that sees a dainty bower
Made in the tree, where she was wont to sit,
   Wonders and sings, but not his power
Who made the arbour: this exceeds her wit.
      But Man doth know
      The spring, whence all things flow: 60

And yet, as though he knew it not,
His knowledge winks, and lets his humours reign;
   They make his life a constant blot,
And all the blood of God to run in vain.
      Ah wretch! what verse
      Can thy strange ways rehearse?

Indeed at first Man was a treasure,
A box of jewels, shop of rarities,
   A ring, whose posy was, *My pleasure*:
He was a garden in a Paradise: 70
      Glory and grace
      Did crown his heart and face.

But sin hath fooled him. Now he is
A lump of flesh, without a foot or wing
   To raise him to a glimpse of bliss:
A sick tossed vessel, dashing on each thing;
      Nay, his own shelf:
      My God, I mean myself.

Jordan (II)

When first my lines of heav'nly joys made mention,
Such was their lustre, they did so excel,
That I sought out quaint words, and trim invention;
My thoughts began to burnish, sprout, and swell,
Curling with metaphors a plain intention,
Decking the sense, as if it were to sell.

Thousands of notions in my brain did run
Off'ring their service, if I were not sped:

I often blotted what I had begun;
This was not quick enough, and that was dead.   10
Nothing could seem too rich to clothe the sun,
Much less those joys which trample on his head.

As flames do work and wind, when they ascend,
So did I weave myself into the sense.
But while I bustled, I might hear a friend
Whisper, *How wide is all this long pretence!*
There is in love a sweetness ready penned:
Copy out only that, and save expense.

Prayer (II)

Of what an easy quick access,
My blessed Lord, art thou! how suddenly
    May our requests thine ear invade!
To show that state dislikes not easiness,
If I but lift mine eyes, my suit is made:
Thou canst no more not hear, than thou canst die.

Of what supreme almighty power
Is thy great arm, which spans the east and west,
    And tacks the centre to the sphere!
By it do all things live their measured hour: 10
We cannot ask the thing, which is not there,
Blaming the shallowness of our request.

Of what unmeasurable love
Art thou possessed, who, when thou couldst not die,
    Wert fain to take our flesh and curse,
And for our sakes in person sin reprove,
That by destroying that which tied thy purse,
Thou mightst make way for liberality!

Since then these three wait on thy throne,
Ease, *Power*, and *Love*; I value prayer so,   20
    That were I to leave all but one,
Wealth, fame, endowments, virtues, all should go;
I and dear prayer would together dwell,
And quickly gain, for each inch lost, an ell.

Obedience

My God, if writings may
Convey a Lordship any way
Whither the buyer and the seller please;
    Let it not thee displease,
If this poor paper do as much as they.

On it my heart doth bleed
As many lines, as there doth need
To pass itself and all it hath to thee.
    To which I do agree,
And here present it as my special Deed.   10

If that hereafter Pleasure
Cavil, and claim her part and measure,
As if this passèd with a reservation,
    Or some such words in fashion;
I here exclude the wrangler from thy treasure.

O let thy sacred will
All thy delight in me fulfil!
Let me not think an action mine own way,
    But as thy love shall sway,
Resigning up the rudder to thy skill.   20

Lord, what is man to thee,
That thou shouldst mind a rotten tree?
Yet since thou canst not choose but see my actions;
    So great are thy perfections,
Thou mayst as well my actions guide, as see.

Besides, thy death and blood
Showed a strange love to all our good:
Thy sorrows were in earnest; no faint proffer,
    Or superficial offer
Of what we might not take, or be withstood.   30

Wherefore I all forgo:
To one word only I say, No:
Where in the Deed there was an intimation
Of a gift or donation,
Lord, let it now by way of purchase go.

He that will pass his land,
As I have mine, may set his hand
And heart unto this Deed, when he hath read;
And make the purchase spread
To both our goods, if he to it will stand.   40

How happy were my part,
If some kind man would thrust his heart
Into these lines; till in heav'n's Court of Rolls
They were by wingèd souls
Entered for both, far above their desert!

Conscience

Peace prattler, do not lour:
Not a fair look, but thou dost call it foul:
Not a sweet dish, but thou dost call it sour:
Music to thee doth howl.
By list'ning to thy chatting fears
I have both lost mine eyes and ears.

Prattler, no more, I say:
My thoughts must work, but like a noiseless sphere;
Harmonious peace must rock them all the day:
No room for prattlers there.   10
If thou persistest, I will tell thee,
That I have physic to expel thee.

And the receipt shall be
My Saviour's blood: whenever at his board
I do but taste it, straight it cleanseth me,
And leaves thee not a word;
No, not a tooth or nail to scratch,
And at my actions carp, or catch.

Yet if thou talkest still,
Besides my physic, know there's some for thee: 20
Some wood and nails to make a staff or bill
            For those that trouble me:
        The bloody cross of my dear Lord
        Is both my physic and my sword.

Sion

Lord, with what glory wast thou served of old,
When Solomon's temple stood and flourishèd!
        Where most things were of purest gold;
        The wood was all embellishèd
With flowers and carvings, mystical and rare:
All showed the builder's, craved the seer's care.

Yet all this glory, all this pomp and state
Did not affect thee much, was not thy aim;
        Something there was, that sowed debate:
        Wherefore thou quitt'st thy ancient claim: 10
And now thy Architecture meets with sin;
For all thy frame and fabric is within.

There thou art struggling with a peevish heart,
Which sometimes crosseth thee, thou sometimes it:
        The fight is hard on either part.
        Great God doth fight, he doth submit.
All Solomon's sea of brass and world of stone
Is not so dear to thee as one good groan.

And truly brass and stones are heavy things,
Tombs for the dead, not temples fit for thee: 20
        But groans are quick, and full of wings,
        And all their motions upward be;
And ever as they mount, like larks they sing;
The note is sad, yet music for a King.

Home

Come Lord, my head doth burn, my heart is sick,
    While thou dost ever, ever stay:
Thy long deferrings wound me to the quick,
    My spirit gaspeth night and day.
        O show thyself to me,
        Or take me up to thee!

How canst thou stay, considering the pace
    The blood did make, which thou didst waste?
When I behold it trickling down thy face,
    I never saw thing make such haste.   10
        O show thyself to me,
        Or take me up to thee!

When man was lost, thy pity looked about
    To see what help in th' earth or sky:
But there was none; at least no help without:
    The help did in thy bosom lie.
        O show thyself to me,
        Or take me up to thee!

There lay thy son: and must he leave that nest,
    That hive of sweetness to remove   20
Thraldom from those, who would not at a feast
    Leave one poor apple for thy love?
        O show thyself to me,
        Or take me up to thee!

He did, he came: O my Redeemer dear,
    After all this canst thou be strange?
So many years baptized, and not appear?
    As if thy love could fail or change.
        O show thyself to me,
        Or take me up to thee!   30

Yet if thou stayest still, why must I stay?
    My God, what is this world to me,
This world of woe? hence all ye clouds, away,

Away; I must get up and see.
    O show thyelf to me,
    Or take me up to thee!

What is this weary world; this meat and drink,
    That chains us by the teeth so fast?
What is this womankind, which I can wink
    Into a blackness and distaste?   40
    O show thyself to me,
    Or take me up to thee!

With one small sigh thou gav'st me th' other day
    I blasted all the joys about me:
And scowling on them as they pined away,
    Now come again, said I, and flout me.
    O show thyself to me,
    Or take me up to thee!

Nothing but drought and dearth, but bush and brake,
    Which way soe'er I look, I see.   50
Some may dream merrily, but when they wake,
    They dress themselves and come to thee.
    O show thyself to me,
    Or take me up to thee!

We talk of harvests; there are no such things,
    But when we leave our corn and hay:
There is no fruitful year, but that which brings
    The last and loved, though dreadful day.
    O show thyself to me,
    Or take me up to thee!   60

Oh loose this frame, this knot of man untie!
    That my free soul may use her wing,
Which now is pinioned with mortality,
    As an entangled, hampered thing.
    O show thyself to me,
    Or take me up to thee!

What have I left, that I should stay and groan?
    The most of me to heav'n is fled:

My thoughts and joys are all packed up and gone,
    And for their old acquaintance plead. 70
        O show thyself to me,
        Or take me up to thee!

Come dearest Lord, pass not this holy season,
    My flesh and bones and joints do pray:
And ev'n my verse, when by the rhyme and reason
    The word is, *Stay*, says ever, *Come*.
        O show thyself to me,
        Or take me up to thee!

The British Church

I joy, dear Mother, when I view
Thy perfect lineaments and hue
        Both sweet and bright.
Beauty in thee takes up her place,
And dates her letters from thy face,
        When she doth write.

A fine aspect in fit array,
Neither too mean, nor yet too gay,
        Shows who is best.
Outlandish looks may not compare: 10
For all they either painted are,
        Or else undressed.

She on the hills, which wantonly
Allureth all in hope to be
        By her preferred,
Hath kissed so long her painted shrines,
That ev'n her face by kissing shines,
        For her reward.

She in the valley is so shy
Of dressing, that her hair doth lie 20
        About her ears:
While she avoids her neighbour's pride,
She wholly goes on th' other side,
        And nothing wears.

But, dearest Mother, what those miss,
The mean, thy praise and glory is,
             And long may be.
Blessed be God, whose love it was
To double-moat thee with his grace,
             And none but thee.　　　　30

The Quip

The merry world did on a day
With his train-bands and mates agree
To meet together, where I lay,
And all in sport to jeer at me.

First, Beauty crept into a rose,
Which when I plucked not, Sir, said she,
Tell me, I pray, Whose hands are those?
But thou shalt answer, Lord, for me.

Then Money came, and chinking still,
What tune is this, poor man? said he:　　10
I heard in music you had skill.
But thou shalt answer, Lord, for me.

Then came brave Glory puffing by
In silks that whistled, who but he?
He scarce allowed me half an eye.
But thou shalt answer, Lord, for me.

Then came quick Wit and Conversation,
And he would needs a comfort be,
And, to be short, make an Oration.
But thou shalt answer, Lord, for me.　　20

Yet when the hour of thy design
To answer these fine things shall come;
Speak not at large; say, I am thine:
And then they have their answer home.

Vanity (II)

Poor silly soul, whose hope and head lies low;
Whose flat delights on earth do creep and grow;
To whom the stars shine not so fair, as eyes;
Nor solid work, as false embroideries;
Hark and beware, lest what you now do measure
And write for sweet, prove a most sour displeasure.
   O hear betimes, lest thy relenting
          May come too late!
   To purchase heaven for repenting
          Is no hard rate.
If souls be made of earthly mould,
      Let them love gold;
      If born on high,
Let them unto their kindred fly:
For they can never be at rest,
Till they regain their ancient nest.
Then silly soul take heed; for earthly joy
Is but a bubble, and makes thee a boy.

The Dawning

Awake sad heart, whom sorrow ever drowns;
  Take up thine eyes, which feed on earth;
Unfold thy forehead gathered into frowns:
  Thy Saviour comes, and with him mirth:
          Awake, awake;
And with a thankful heart his comforts take.
  But thou dost still lament, and pine, and cry;
  And feel his death, but not his victory.

Arise sad heart; if thou do not withstand,
  Christ's resurrection thine may be:
Do not by hanging down break from the hand,
  Which as it riseth, raiseth thee:
          Arise, arise;
And with his burial-linen dry thine eyes:
  Christ left his grave-clothes, that we might, when grief
  Draws tears, or blood, not want a handkerchief.

JESU

JESU is in my heart, his sacred name
Is deeply carvèd there: but th'other week
A great affliction broke the little frame,
Ev'n all to pieces: which I went to seek:
And first I found the corner, where was *J*,
After, where *ES*, and next where *U* was graved.
When I had got these parcels, instantly
I sat me down to spell them, and perceived
That to my broken heart he was *I ease you*,
       And to my whole is *JESU*.   10

Business

    Canst be idle? canst thou play,
    Foolish soul who sinned today?

Rivers run, and springs each one
Know their home, and get them gone:
Hast thou tears, or hast thou none?

If, poor soul, thou hast no tears,
Would thou hadst no faults or fears!
Who hath these, those ill forbears.

Winds still work: it is their plot,
Be the season cold, or hot: 10
Hast thou sighs, or hast thou not?

If thou hast no sighs or groans,
Would thou hadst no flesh and bones!
Lesser pains 'scape greater ones.

    But if yet thou idle be,
    Foolish soul, Who died for thee?

Who did leave his Father's throne,
To assume thy flesh and bone;
Had he life, or had he none?

If he had not lived for thee, 20
Thou hadst died most wretchedly;
And two deaths had been thy fee.

He so far thy good did plot,
That his own self he forgot.
Did he die, or did he not?

If he had not died for thee,
Thou hadst lived in misery.
Two lives worse than ten deaths be.

And hath any space of breath
'Twixt his sins and Saviour's death? 30

He that loseth gold, though dross,
Tells to all he meets, his cross:
He that sins, hath he no loss?

He that finds a silver vein,
Thinks on it, and thinks again:
Brings thy Saviour's death no gain?

Who in heart not ever kneels,
Neither sin nor Saviour feels.

Dialogue

Sweetest Saviour, if my soul
    Were but worth the having,
Quickly should I then control
    Any thought of waving.
But when all my care and pains
Cannot give the name of gains
To thy wretch so full of stains,
What delight or hope remains?

What, Child, is the balance thine,
    Thine the poise and measure?   10
If I say, Thou shalt be mine;
    Finger not my treasure.
What the gains in having thee
Do amount to, only he,
Who for man was sold, can see;
That transferred th' accounts to me.

But as I can see no merit,
    Leading to this favour:
So the way to fit me for it
    Is beyond my savour.   20
As the reason then is thine;
So the way is none of mine:
I disclaim the whole design:
Sin disclaims and I resign.

That is all, if that I could
    Get without repining;
And my clay, my creature, would
    Follow my resigning:
That as I did freely part
With my glory and desert,   30
Left all joys to feel all smart——
    Ah! no more: thou break'st my heart.

Dullness

Why do I languish thus, drooping and dull,
        As if I were all earth?
O give me quickness, that I may with mirth
        Praise thee brim-full!

The wanton lover in a curious strain
        Can praise his fairest fair;
And with quaint metaphors her curlèd hair
        Curl o'er again.

Thou art my loveliness, my life, my light,
                    Beauty alone to me: 10
Thy bloody death and undeserved, makes thee
                    Pure red and white.

When all perfections as but one appear,
                    That those thy form doth show,
The very dust, where thou dost tread and go,
                    Makes beauties here.

Where are my lines then? my approaches? views?
                    Where are my window-songs?
Lovers are still pretending, and ev'n wrongs
                    Sharpen their Muse: 20

But I am lost in flesh, whose sugared lies
                    Still mock me, and grow bold:
Sure thou didst put a mind there, if I could
                    Find where it lies.

Lord, clear thy gift, that with a constant wit
                    I may but look towards thee:
Look only; for to *love* thee, who can be,
                    What angel fit?

Love-joy

As on a window late I cast mine eye,
I saw a vine drop grapes with *J* and *C*
Annealed on every bunch. One standing by
Asked what it meant. I, who am never loth
To spend my judgement, said, It seemed to me
To be the body and the letters both
Of *Joy* and *Charity*. Sir, you have not missed,
The man replied; it figures *JESUS CHRIST*.

Providence

O sacred Providence, who from end to end
Strongly and sweetly movest, shall I write,
And not of thee, through whom my fingers bend
To hold my quill? shall they not do thee right?

Of all the creatures both in sea and land
Only to Man thou hast made known thy ways,
And put the pen alone into his hand,
And made him Secretary of thy praise.

Beasts fain would sing; birds ditty to their notes;
Trees would be tuning on their native lute   10
To thy renown: but all their hands and throats
Are brought to Man, while they are lame and mute.

Man is the world's high priest: he doth present
The sacrifice for all; while they below
Unto the service mutter an assent,
Such as springs use that fall, and winds that blow.

He that to praise and laud thee doth refrain,
Doth not refrain unto himself alone,
But robs a thousand who would praise thee fain,
And doth commit a world of sin in one.   20

The beasts say, Eat me: but, if beasts must teach,
The tongue is yours to eat, but mine to praise.
The trees say, Pull me: but the hand you stretch,
Is mine to write, as it is yours to raise.

Wherefore, most sacred Spirit, I here present
For me and all my fellows praise to thee:
And just it is that I should pay the rent,
Because the benefit accrues to me.

We all acknowledge both thy power and love
To be exact, transcendent, and divine;   30
Who dost so strongly and so sweetly move,
While all things have their will, yet none but thine.

For either thy command or thy permission
Lay hands on all: they are thy right and left.
The first puts on with speed and expedition;
The other curbs sin's stealing pace and theft.

Nothing escapes them both; all must appear,
And be disposed, and dressed, and tuned by thee,
Who sweetly temper'st all. If we could hear
Thy skill and art, what music would it be!   40

Thou art in small things great, not small in any:
Thy even praise can neither rise, nor fall.
Thou art in all things one, in each thing many:
For thou art infinite in one and all.

Tempests are calm to thee; they know thy hand,
And hold it fast, as children do their fathers,
Which cry and follow. Thou hast made poor sand
Check the proud sea, ev'n when it swells and gathers.

Thy cupboard serves the world: the meat is set,
Where all may reach: no beast but knows his feed.   50
Birds teach us hawking; fishes have their net:
The great prey on the less, they on some weed.

Nothing engendered doth prevent his meat:
Flies have their table spread, ere they appear.
Some creatures have in winter what to eat;
Others do sleep, and envy not their cheer.

How finely dost thou times and seasons spin,
And make a twist checkered with night and day!
Which as it lengthens winds, and winds us in,
As bowls go on, but turning all the way.   60

Each creature hath a wisdom for his good.
The pigeons feed their tender offspring, crying,
When they are callow; but withdraw their food
When they are fledge, that need may teach them flying.

Bees work for man; and yet they never bruise
Their master's flower, but leave it, having done,
As fair as ever, and as fit to use;
So both the flower doth stay, and honey run.

Sheep eat the grass, and dung the ground for more:
Trees after bearing drop their leaves for soil: 70
Springs vent their streams, and by expense get store:
Clouds cool by heat, and baths by cooling boil.

Who hath the virtue to express the rare
And curious virtues both of herbs and stones?
Is there an herb for that? O that thy care
Would show a root, that gives expressions!

And if an herb hath power, what have the stars?
A rose, besides his beauty, is a cure.
Doubtless our plagues and plenty, peace and wars
Are there much surer than our art is sure.   80

Thou hast hid metals: man may take them thence;
But at his peril: when he digs the place,
He makes a grave; as if the thing had sense,
And threatened man, that he should fill the space.

Ev'n poisons praise thee. Should a thing be lost?
Should creatures want for want of heed their due?
Since where are poisons, antidotes are most:
The help stands close, and keeps the fear in view.

The sea, which seems to stop the traveller,
Is by a ship the speedier passage made.   90
The winds, who think they rule the mariner,
Are ruled by him, and taught to serve his trade.

And as thy house is full, so I adore
Thy curious art in marshalling thy goods.
The hills with health abound; the vales with store;
The South with marble; North with furs and woods.

Hard things are glorious; easy things good cheap.
The common all men have; that which is rare
Men therefore seek to have, and care to keep.
The healthy frosts with summer-fruits compare. 100

Light without wind is glass: warm without weight
Is wool and fur: cool without closeness, shade:
Speed without pains, a horse: tall without height,
A servile hawk: low without loss, a spade.

All countries have enough to serve their need:
If they seek fine things, thou dost make them run
For their offence; and then dost turn their speed
To be commerce and trade from sun to sun.

Nothing wears clothes, but Man; nothing doth need
But he to wear them. Nothing useth fire, 110
But Man alone, to show his heav'nly breed:
And only he hath fuel in desire.

When th' earth was dry, thou mad'st a sea of wet:
When that lay gathered, thou didst broach the mountains:
When yet some places could no moisture get,
The winds grew gard'ners, and the clouds good fountains.

Rain, do not hurt my flowers; but gently spend
Your honey drops: press not to smell them here:
When they are ripe, their odour will ascend,
And at your lodging with their thanks appear. 120

How harsh are thorns to pears! and yet they make
A better hedge, and need less reparation.
How smooth are silks compared with a stake,
Or with a stone! yet make no good foundation.

Sometimes thou dost divide thy gifts to man,
Sometimes unite. The Indian nut alone
Is clothing, meat and trencher, drink and can,
Boat, cable, sail and needle, all in one.

Most herbs that grow in brooks, are hot and dry.
Cold fruits warm kernels help against the wind.   130
The lemon's juice and rind cure mutually.
The whey of milk doth loose, the milk doth bind.

Thy creatures leap not, but express a feast,
Where all the guests sit close, and nothing wants.
Frogs marry fish and flesh; bats, bird and beast;
Sponges, nonsense and sense; mines, th' earth and plants.

To show thou art not bound, as if thy lot
Were worse than ours, sometimes thou shiftest hands.
Most things move th' under-jaw; the crocodile not.
Most things sleep lying; th' elephant leans or stands.   140

But who hath praise enough? nay, who hath any?
None can express thy works, but he that knows them:
And none can know thy works, which are so many,
And so complete, but only he that owes them.

All things that are, though they have sev'ral ways,
Yet in their being join with one advice
To honour thee: and so I give thee praise
In all my other hymns, but in this twice.

Each thing that is, although in use and name
It go for one, hath many ways in store   150
To honour thee; and so each hymn thy fame
Extolleth many ways, yet this one more.

Hope

I gave to Hope a watch of mine: but he
    An anchor gave to me.
Then an old prayer-book I did present:
    And he an optic sent.
With that I gave a vial full of tears:
    But he a few green ears.
Ah Loiterer! I'll no more, no more I'll bring:
    I did expect a ring.

Sin's Round

Sorry I am, my God, sorry I am,
That my offences course it in a ring.
My thoughts are working like a busy flame,
Until their cockatrice they hatch and bring:
And when they once have perfected their draughts,
My words take fire from my inflamèd thoughts.

My words take fire from my inflamèd thoughts,
Which spit it forth like the Sicilian Hill.
They vent the wares, and pass them with their faults,
And by their breathing ventilate the ill.   10
But words suffice not, where are lewd intentions:
My hands do join to finish the inventions.

My hands do join to finish the inventions:
And so my sins ascend three stories high,
As Babel grew, before there were dissensions.
Yet ill deeds loiter not: for they supply
New thoughts of sinning: wherefore, to my shame,
Sorry I am, my God, sorry I am.

Time

Meeting with Time, Slack thing, said I,
Thy scythe is dull; whet it for shame.
No marvel Sir, he did reply,
If it at length deserve some blame:
    But where one man would have me grind it,
    Twenty for one too sharp do find it.

Perhaps some such of old did pass,
Who above all things loved this life;
To whom thy scythe a hatchet was,
Which now is but a pruning-knife.   10
    Christ's coming hath made man thy debtor,
    Since by thy cutting he grows better.

And in his blessing thou art blest:
For where thou only wert before
An executioner at best;
Thou art a gard'ner now, and more,
  An usher to convey our souls
  Beyond the utmost stars and poles.

And this is that makes life so long,
While it detains us from our God. 20
Ev'n pleasures here increase the wrong,
And length of days lengthen the rod.
  Who wants the place, where God doth dwell,
  Partakes already half of hell.

Of what strange length must that needs be,
Which ev'n eternity excludes!
Thus far Time heard me patiently:
Then chafing said, This man deludes:
  What do I here before his door?
  He doth not crave less time, but more. 30

Gratefulness

Thou that hast giv'n so much to me,
Give one thing more, a grateful heart.
See how thy beggar works on thee
      By art.

He makes thy gifts occasion more,
And says, If he in this be crossed,
All thou hast giv'n him heretofore
      Is lost.

But thou didst reckon, when at first
Thy word our hearts and hands did crave, 10
What it would come to at the worst
      To save.

Perpetual knockings at thy door,
Tears sullying thy transparent rooms,
Gift upon gift, much would have more,
        And comes.

This notwithstanding, thou wentst on,
And didst allow us all our noise:
Nay, thou hast made a sigh and groan,
        Thy joys.   20

Not that thou hast not still above
Much better tunes, than groans can make;
But that these country-airs thy love
        Did take.

Wherefore I cry, and cry again;
And in no quiet canst thou be,
Till I a thankful heart obtain
        Of thee:

Not thankful, when it pleaseth me;
As if thy blessings had spare days:
But such a heart, whose pulse may be   30
        Thy praise.

Peace

Sweet Peace, where dost thou dwell? I humbly crave,
        Let me once know.
  I sought thee in a secret cave,
        And asked, if Peace were there.
A hollow wind did seem to answer, No:
        Go seek elsewhere.

I did; and going did a rainbow note:
        Surely, thought I,
  This is the lace of Peace's coat:
        I will search out the matter.   10
But while I looked, the clouds immediately
        Did break and scatter.

Then went I to a garden, and did spy
        A gallant flower,
  The Crown Imperial: Sure, said I,
        Peace at the root must dwell.
But when I digged, I saw a worm dèvour
        What showed so well.

At length I met a rev'rend good old man,
        Whom when for Peace   20
  I did demand, he thus began:
        There was a Prince of old
At Salem dwelt, who lived with good increase
        Of flock and fold.

He sweetly lived; yet sweetness did not save
        His life from foes.
  But after death out of his grave
        There sprang twelve stalks of wheat:
Which many wond'ring at, got some of those
        To plant and set.   30

It prospered strangely, and did soon disperse
        Through all the earth:
  For they that taste it do rehearse,
        That virtue lies therein,
A secret virtue bringing peace and mirth
        By flight of sin.

Take of this grain, which in my garden grows,
        And grows for you;
  Make bread of it: and that repose
        And peace, which ev'rywhere   40
With so much earnestness you do pursue,
        Is only there.

Confession

O what a cunning guest
Is this same grief! within my heart I made
    Closets; and in them many a chest;
    And, like a master in my trade,
In those chests, boxes; in each box, a till:
Yet grief knows all, and enters when he will.

    No screw, no piercer can
Into a piece of timber work and wind,
    As God's afflictions into man,
    When he a torture hath designed.
They are too subtle for the subtlest hearts;
And fall, like rheums, upon the tend'rest parts.

    We are the earth; and they,
Like moles within us, heave, and cast about:
    And till they foot and clutch their prey,
    They never cool, much less give out.
No smith can make such locks but they have keys:
Closets are halls to them; and hearts, highways.

    Only an open breast
Doth shut them out, so that they cannot enter;
    Or, if they enter, cannot rest,
    But quickly seek some new adventure.
Smooth open hearts no fast'ning have; but fiction
Doth give a hold and handle to affliction.

    Wherefore my faults and sins,
Lord, I acknowledge; take thy plagues away:
    For since confession pardon wins,
    I challenge here the brightest day,
The clearest diamond: let them do their best,
They shall be thick and cloudy to my breast.

Giddiness

Oh, what a thing is man! how far from power,
        From settled peace and rest!
He is some twenty sev'ral men at least
        Each sev'ral hour.

One while he counts of heav'n, as of his treasure:
        But then a thought creeps in,
And calls him coward, who for fear of sin
        Will lose a pleasure.

Now he will fight it out, and to the wars;
        Now eat his bread in peace,   10
And snudge in quiet: now he scorns increase;
        Now all day spares.

He builds a house, which quickly down must go,
        As if a whirlwind blew
And crushed the building: and it's partly true,
        His mind is so.

O what a sight were Man, if his attires
        Did alter with his mind;
And like a dolphin's skin, his clothes combined
        With his desires!   20

Surely if each one saw another's heart,
        There would be no commerce,
No sale or bargain pass: all would disperse,
        And live apart.

Lord, mend or rather make us: one creation
        Will not suffice our turn:
Except thou make us daily, we shall spurn
        Our own salvation.

The Bunch of Grapes

Joy, I did lock thee up: but some bad man
    Hath let thee out again:
And now, methinks, I am where I began
    Sev'n years ago: one vogue and vein,
    One air of thoughts usurps my brain.
I did towards Canaan draw; but now I am
Brought back to the Red Sea, the sea of shame.

For as the Jews of old by God's command
    Travelled, and saw no town;
So now each Christian hath his journeys spanned: 10
    Their story pens and sets us down.
    A single deed is small renown.
God's works are wide, and let in future times;
His ancient justice overflows our crimes.

Then have we too our guardian fires and clouds;
    Our Scripture-dew drops fast:
We have our sands and serpents, tents and shrouds;
    Alas! our murmurings come not last.
    But where's the cluster? where's the taste
Of mine inheritance? Lord, if I must borrow,   20
Let me as well take up their joy, as sorrow.

But can he want the grape, who hath the wine?
    I have their fruit and more.
Blessèd be God, who prospered Noah's vine,
    And made it bring forth grapes good store.
    But much more him I must adore,
Who of the Law's sour juice sweet wine did make,
Ev'n God himself being pressèd for my sake.

Love Unknown

Dear Friend, sit down, the tale is long and sad:
And in my faintings I presume your love
Will more comply than help. A Lord I had,
And have, of whom some grounds, which may improve,

I hold for two lives, and both lives in me.
To him I brought a dish of fruit one day,
And in the middle placed my heart. But he
                    (I sigh to say)
Looked on a servant, who did know his eye
Better than you know me, or (which is one)   10
Than I myself. The servant instantly
Quitting the fruit, seized on my heart alone,
And threw it in a font, wherein did fall
A stream of blood, which issued from the side
Of a great rock: I well remember all,
And have good cause: there it was dipped and dyed,
And washed, and wrung: the very wringing yet
Enforceth tears. *Your heart was foul, I fear.*
Indeed 'tis true. I did and do commit
Many a fault more than my lease will bear;   20
Yet still asked pardon, and was not denied.
But you shall hear. After my heart was well,
And clean and fair, as I one even-tide
                    (I sigh to tell)
Walked by myself abroad, I saw a large
And spacious furnace flaming, and thereon
A boiling cauldron, round about whose verge
Was in great letters set *AFFLICTION.*
The greatness showed the owner. So I went
To fetch a sacrifice out of my fold,   30
Thinking with that, which I did thus present,
To warm his love, which I did fear grew cold.
But as my heart did tender it, the man,
Who was to take it from me, slipped his hand,
And threw my heart into the scalding pan;
My heart, that brought it (do you understand?)
The offerer's heart. *Your heart was hard, I fear.*
Indeed it's true. I found a callous matter
Began to spread and to expatiate there:
But with a richer drug than scalding water   40
I bathed it often, ev'n with holy blood,
Which at a board, while many drunk bare wine,
A friend did steal into my cup for good,
Ev'n taken inwardly, and most divine
To supple hardnesses. But at the length

Out of the cauldron getting, soon I fled
Unto my house, where to repair the strength
Which I had lost, I hasted to my bed.
But when I thought to sleep out all these faults
    (I sigh to speak)   50
I found that some had stuffed the bed with thoughts,
I would say *thorns*. Dear, could my heart not break,
When with my pleasures ev'n my rest was gone?
Full well I understood, who had been there:
For I had giv'n the key to none, but one:
It must be he. *Your heart was dull, I fear.*
Indeed a slack and sleepy state of mind
Did oft possess me, so that when I prayed,
Though my lips went, my heart did stay behind.
But all my scores were by another paid,   60
Who took the debt upon him. *Truly, Friend,*
For ought I hear, your Master shows to you
More favour than you wot of. Mark the end.
The Font did only, what was old, renew:
The Cauldron suppled, what was grown too hard:
The Thorns did quicken, what was grown too dull:
All did but strive to mend, what you had marred.
Wherefore be cheered, and praise him to the full
Each day, each hour, each moment of the week,
Who fain would have you be new, tender, quick. 70

Man's Medley

Hark, how the birds do sing,
    And woods do ring.
All creatures have their joy: and man hath his.
    Yet if we rightly measure,
      Man's joy and pleasure
Rather hereafter, than in present, is.

    To this life things of sense
      Make their pretence:
In th' other angels have a right by birth:
    Man ties them both alone,
      And makes them one,   10
With th' one hand touching heav'n, with th' other earth.

In soul he mounts and flies,
In flesh he dies.
He wears a stuff whose thread is coarse and round,
But trimmed with curious lace,
And should take place
After the trimming, not the stuff and ground.

Not that he may not here
Taste of the cheer,   20
But as birds drink, and straight lift up their head,
So he must sip and think
Of better drink
He may attain to, after he is dead.

But as his joys are double;
So is his trouble.
He hath two winters, other things but one:
Both frosts and thoughts do nip,
And bite his lip;
And he of all things fears two deaths alone.   30

Yet ev'n the greatest griefs
May be reliefs,
Could he but take them right, and in their ways.
Happy is he, whose heart
Hath found the art
To turn his double pains to double praise.

The Storm

If as the winds and waters here below
Do fly and flow,
My sighs and tears as busy were above;
Sure they would move
And much affect thee, as tempestuous times
Amuse poor mortals, and object their crimes.

Stars have their storms, ev'n in a high degree,
          As well as we.
A throbbing conscience spurrèd by remorse
          Hath a strange force: 10
It quits the earth, and mounting more and more
Dares to assault thee, and besiege thy door.

There it stands knocking, to thy music's wrong,
          And drowns the song.
Glory and honour are set by, till it
          An answer get.
Poets have wronged poor storms: such days are best;
They purge the air without, within the breast.

Paradise

I bless thee, Lord, because I GROW
Among thy trees, which in a ROW
To thee both fruit and order OW.

What open force, or hidden CHARM
Can blast my fruit, or bring me HARM,
While the inclosure is thine ARM?

Inclose me still for fear I START.
Be to me rather sharp and TART,
Than let me want thy hand and ART.

When thou dost greater judgements SPARE,   10
And with thy knife but prune and PARE,
Ev'n fruitful trees more fruitful ARE.

Such sharpness shows the sweetest FREND:
Such cuttings rather heal than REND:
And such beginnings touch their END.

The Method

Poor heart, lament.
For since thy God refuseth still,
There is some rub, some discontent,
Which cools his will.

Thy Father could
Quickly effect, what thou dost move;
For he is *Power*: and sure he would;
For he is *Love*.

Go search this thing,
Tumble thy breast, and turn thy book.   10
If thou hadst lost a glove or ring,
Wouldst thou not look?

What do I see
Written above there? *Yesterday*
I did behave me carelessly,
When I did pray.

And should God's ear
To such indifferents chainèd be,
Who do not their own motions hear?
Is God less free?   20

But stay! what's there?
Late when I would have something done,
I had a motion to forbear,
Yet I went on.

And should God's ear,
Which needs not man, be tied to those
Who hear not him, but quickly hear
His utter foes?

Then once more pray:
Down with thy knees, up with thy voice.   30
Seek pardon first, and God will say,
Glad heart rejoice.

Divinity

As men, for fear the stars should sleep and nod,
　　And trip at night, have spheres supplied;
As if a star were duller than a clod,
　　Which knows his way without a guide:

Just so the other heav'n they also serve,
　　Divinity's transcendent sky:
Which with the edge of wit they cut and carve.
　　Reason triumphs, and faith lies by.

Could not that Wisdom, which first broached the wine,
　　Have thickened it with definitions? 10
And jagged his seamless coat, had that been fine,
　　With curious questions and divisions?

But all the doctrine, which he taught and gave,
　　Was clear as heav'n, from whence it came.
At least those beams of truth, which only save,
　　Surpass in brightness any flame.

Love God, and love your neighbour. Watch and pray.
　　Do as ye would be done unto.
O dark instructions; ev'n as dark as day!
　　Who can these Gordian knots undo? 20

But he doth bid us take his blood for wine.
　　Bid what he please; yet I am sure,
To take and taste what he doth there design,
　　Is all that saves, and not obscure.

Then burn thy Epicycles, foolish man;
　　Break all thy spheres, and save thy head.
Faith needs no staff of flesh, but stoutly can
　　To heav'n alone both go, and lead.

Ephes. 4. 30
Grieve not the Holy Spirit, etc.

And art thou grievèd, sweet and sacred Dove,
      When I am sour,
      And cross thy love?
Grievèd for me? the God of strength and power
      Grieved for a worm, which when I tread,
      I pass away and leave it dead?

Then weep mine eyes, the God of love doth grieve:
      Weep foolish heart,
      And weeping live:
For death is dry as dust. Yet if ye part,   10
      End as the night, whose sable hue
      Your sins express; melt into dew.

When saucy mirth shall knock or call at door,
      Cry out, Get hence,
      Or cry no more.
Almighty God doth grieve, he puts on sense:
      I sin not to my grief alone,
      But to my God's too; he doth groan:

Oh take thy lute, and tune it to a strain,
      Which may with thee   20
      All day complain.
There can no discord but in ceasing be.
      Marbles can weep; and surely strings
      More bowels have, than such hard things.

Lord, I adjudge myself to tears and grief,
      Ev'n endless tears
      Without relief.
If a clear spring for me no time forbears,
      But runs, although I be not dry;
      I am no crystal, what shall I?   30

Yet if I wail not still, since still to wail
   Nature denies;
   And flesh would fail,
If my deserts were masters of mine eyes:
   Lord, pardon, for thy Son makes good
   My want of tears with store of blood.

The Family

What doth this noise of thoughts within my heart,
   As if they had a part?
What do these loud complaints and puling fears,
  As if there were no rule or ears?

But, Lord, the house and family are thine,
   Though some of them repine.
Turn out these wranglers, which defile thy seat:
  For where thou dwellest all is neat.

First Peace and Silence all disputes control,
   Then Order plays the soul;   10
And giving all things their set forms and hours,
  Makes of wild woods sweet walks and bowers.

Humble Obedience near the door doth stand,
   Expecting a command:
Than whom in waiting nothing seems more slow,
  Nothing more quick when she doth go.

Joys oft are there, and griefs as oft as joys;
   But griefs without a noise:
Yet speak they louder than distempered fears.
  What is so shrill as silent tears?   20

This is thy house, with these it doth abound:
   And where these are not found,
Perhaps thou com'st sometimes, and for a day;
  But not to make a constant stay.

The Size

    Content thee, greedy heart.
Modest and moderate joys to those, that have
Title to more hereafter when they part,
        Are passing brave.
    Let th' upper springs into the low
    Descend and fall, and thou dost flow.

    What though some have a fraught
Of cloves and nutmegs, and in cinnamon sail;
If thou hast wherewithal to spice a draught,
        When griefs prevail;   10
    And for the future time art heir
    To th' Isle of spices, is't not fair?

    To be in both worlds full
Is more than God was, who was hungry here.
Wouldst thou his laws of fasting disannul?
        Exact good cheer?
    Lay out thy joy, yet hope to save it?
    Wouldst thou both eat thy cake, and have it?

    Great joys are all at once;
But little do reserve themselves for more: 20
Those have their hopes; these what they have renounce,
        And live on score:
    Those are at home; these journey still,
    And meet the rest on Sion's hill.

    Thy Saviour sentenced joy,
And in the flesh condemned it as unfit,
At least in lump: for such doth oft destroy;
        Whereas a bit
    Doth 'tice us on to hopes of more,
    And for the present health restore.   30

    A Christian's state and case
Is not a corpulent, but a thin and spare,
Yet active strength: whose long and bony face

      Content and care
Do seem to equally divide,
Like a pretender, not a bride.

      Wherefore sit down, good heart;
Grasp not at much, for fear thou losest all.
If comforts fell according to desert,
      They would great frosts and snows destroy: 40
      For we should count, Since the last joy.

      Then close again the seam,
Which thou hast opened: do not spread thy robe
In hope of great things. Call to mind thy dream,
         An earthly globe,
      On whose meridian was engraven,
      These seas are tears, and heav'n the haven.

Artillery

As I one ev'ning sat before my cell,
Me thoughts a star did shoot into my lap.
I rose, and shook my clothes, as knowing well,
That from small fires comes oft no small mishap.
      When suddenly I heard one say,
      Do as thou usest, disobey,
      Expel good motions from thy breast,
Which have the face of fire, but end in rest.

I, who had heard of music in the spheres,
But not of speech in stars, began to muse: 10
But turning to my God, whose ministers
The stars and all things are; If I refuse,
      Dread Lord, said I, so oft my good;
      Then I refuse not ev'n with blood
      To wash away my stubborn thought:
For I will do or suffer what I ought.

But I have also stars and shooters too,
Born where thy servants both artilleries use.
My tears and prayers night and day do woo,

And work up to thee; yet thou dost refuse.   20
    Not but I am (I must say still)
    Much more obliged to do thy will,
    Than thou to grant mine: but because
Thy promise now hath ev'n set thee thy laws.

Then we are shooters both, and thou dost deign
To enter combat with us, and contest
With thine own clay. But I would parley fain:
Shun not my arrows, and behold my breast.
    Yet if thou shunnest, I am thine:
    I must be so, if I am mine.   30
    There is no articling with thee:
I am but finite, yet thine infinitely.

Church-rents and Schisms

Brave rose, (alas!) where art thou? in the chair
Where thou didst lately so triumph and shine
A worm doth sit, whose many feet and hair
Are the more foul, the more thou wert divine.
This, this hath done it, this did bite the root
And bottom of the leaves: which when the wind
Did once perceive, it blew them under foot,
Where rude unhallowed steps do crush and grind
    Their beauteous glories. Only shreds of thee,
    And those all bitten, in thy chair I see.   10

Why doth my Mother blush? is she the rose,
And shows it so? Indeed Christ's precious blood
Gave you a colour once; which when your foes
Thought to let out, the bleeding did you good,
And made you look much fresher than before.
But when debates and fretting jealousies
Did worm and work within you more and more,
Your colour faded, and calamities
    Turnèd your ruddy into pale and bleak:
    Your health and beauty both began to break.   20

Then did your sev'ral parts unloose and start:
Which when your neighbours saw, like a north wind
They rushèd in, and cast them in the dirt
Where Pagans tread. O Mother dear and kind,
Where shall I get me eyes enough to weep,
As many eyes as stars? since it is night,
And much of Asia and Europe fast asleep,
And ev'n all Afric'; would at least I might
    With these two poor ones lick up all the dew,
    Which falls by night, and pour it out for you!   30

Justice (II)

O dreadful Justice, what a fright and terror
        Wast thou of old,
        When sin and error
    Did show and shape thy looks to me,
     And through their glass discolour thee!
He that did but look up, was proud and bold.

The dishes of thy balance seemed to gape,
        Like two great pits;
        The beam and scape
    Did like some torturing engine show;   10
     Thy hand above did burn and glow,
Daunting the stoutest hearts, the proudest wits.

But now that Christ's pure veil presents the sight,
        I see no fears:
        Thy hand is white,
    Thy scales like buckets, which attend
     And interchangeably descend,
Lifting to heaven from this well of tears.

For where before thou still didst call on me,
        Now I still touch   20
        And harp on thee.
    God's promises have made thee mine;
     Why should I justice now decline?
Against me there is none, but for me much.

The Pilgrimage

I travelled on, seeing the hill, where lay
        My expectation.
  A long it was and weary way.
    The gloomy cave of Desperation
I left on th' one, and on the other side
        The rock of Pride.

And so I came to Fancy's meadow strowed
        With many a flower:
    Fain would I here have made abode,
    But I was quickened by my hour.   10
So to Care's copse I came, and there got through
        With much ado.

That led me to the wild of Passion, which
        Some call the wold;
    A wasted place, but sometimes rich.
    Here I was robbed of all my gold,
Save one good Angel, which a friend had tied
        Close to my side.

At length I got unto the gladsome hill,
        Where lay my hope,   20
    Where lay my heart; and climbing still,
    When I had gained the brow and top,
A lake of brackish waters on the ground
        Was all I found.

With that abashed and struck with many a sting
        Of swarming fears,
    I fell, and cried, Alas my King!
    Can both the way and end be tears?
Yet taking heart I rose, and then perceived
        I was deceived: 30

My hill was further: so I flung away,
        Yet heard a cry,
    Just as I went, *None goes that way*
    And lives: If that be all, said I,
After so foul a journey death is fair,
        And but a chair.

The Holdfast

I threatened to observe the strict decree
    Of my dear God with all my power and might.
    But I was told by one, it could not be;
Yet I might trust in God to be my light.
Then will I trust, said I, in him alone.
    Nay, ev'n to trust in him, was also his:
    We must confess that nothing is our own.
Then I confess that he my succour is:
But to have nought is ours, not to confess
    That we have nought. I stood amazed at this,   10
    Much troubled, till I heard a friend express,
That all things were more ours by being his.
    What Adam had, and forfeited for all,
    Christ keepeth now, who cannot fail or fall.

Complaining

    Do not beguile my heart,
        Because thou art
My power and wisdom. Put me not to shame,
        Because I am
    Thy clay that weeps, thy dust that calls.

    Thou art the Lord of glory;
        The deed and story
Are both thy due: but I a silly fly,
        That live or die
    According as the weather falls.   10

    Art thou all justice, Lord?
        Shows not thy word
More attributes? Am I all throat or eye,
        To weep or cry?
    Have I no parts but those of grief?

Let not thy wrathful power
Afflict my hour,
My inch of life: or let thy gracious power
Contract my hour,
That I may climb and find relief.   20

The Discharge

Busy enquiring heart, what wouldst thou know?
Why dost thou pry,
And turn, and leer, and with a lickerous eye
Look high and low;
And in thy lookings stretch and grow?

Hast thou not made thy counts, and summed up all?
Did not thy heart
Give up the whole, and with the whole depart?
Let what will fall:
That which is past who can recall?   10

Thy life is God's, thy time to come is gone,
And is his right.
He is thy night at noon: he is at night
Thy noon alone.
The crop is his, for he hath sown.

And well it was for thee, when this befell,
That God did make
Thy business his, and in thy life partake:
For thou canst tell,
If it be his once, all is well.   20

Only the present is thy part and fee.
And happy thou,
If, though thou didst not beat thy future brow,
Thou couldst well see
What present things required of thee.

They ask enough; why shouldst thou further go?
              Raise not the mud
Of future depths, but drink the clear and good.
              Dig not for woe
    In times to come; for it will grow.   30

Man and the present fit: if he provide,
              He breaks the square.
This hour is mine: if for the next I care,
              I grow too wide,
    And do encroach upon death's side.

For death each hour environs and surrounds.
              He that would know
And care for future chances, cannot go
              Unto those grounds,
    But through a church-yard which them bounds.   40

Things present shrink and die: but they that spend
              Their thoughts and sense
On future grief, do not remove it thence,
              But it extend,
    And draw the bottom out an end.

God chains the dog till night: wilt loose the chain,
              And wake thy sorrow?
Wilt thou forestall it, and now grieve tomorrow,
              And then again
    Grieve over freshly all thy pain?   50

Either grief will not come: or if it must,
              Do not forecast.
And while it cometh, it is almost past.
              Away distrust:
    My God hath promised; he is just.

Praise (II)

King of Glory, King of Peace,
      I will love thee:
And that love may never cease,
      I will move thee.

Thou hast granted my request,
      Thou hast heard me:
Thou didst note my working breast,
      Thou hast spared me.

Wherefore with my utmost art
      I will sing thee,   10
And the cream of all my heart
      I will bring thee.

Though my sins against me cried,
      Thou didst clear me;
And alone, when they replied,
      Thou didst hear me.

Sev'n whole days, not one in seven,
      I will praise thee.
In my heart, though not in heaven,
      I can raise thee.   20

Thou grew'st soft and moist with tears,
      Thou relentedst:
And when Justice called for fears,
      Thou dissentedst.

Small it is, in this poor sort
      To enrol thee:
Ev'n eternity is too short
      To extol thee.

An Offering

Come, bring thy gift. If blessings were as slow
As men's returns, what would become of fools?
What hast thou there? a heart? but is it pure?
Search well and see; for hearts have many holes.
Yet one pure heart is nothing to bestow:
In Christ two natures met to be thy cure.

O that within us hearts had propagation,
Since many gifts do challenge many hearts!
Yet one, if good, may title to a number;
And single things grow fruitful by deserts.   10
In public judgements one may be a nation,
And fence a plague, while others sleep and slumber.

But all I fear is lest thy heart displease,
As neither good, nor one: so oft divisions
Thy lusts have made, and not thy lusts alone;
Thy passions also have their set partitions.
These parcel out thy heart: recover these,
And thou mayst offer many gifts in one.

There is a balsam, or indeed a blood,
Dropping from heav'n, which doth both cleanse and close   20
All sorts of wounds; of such strange force it is.
Seek out this All-heal, and seek no repose,
Until thou find and use it to thy good:
Then bring thy gift, and let thy hymn be this:

Since my sadness
Into gladness
Lord thou dost convert,
O accept
What thou hast kept,
As thy due desert.   30

Had I many,
Had I any,
(For this heart is none)

All were thine
And none of mine:
Surely thine alone.

Yet thy favour
May give savour
To this poor oblation;
And it raise   40
To be thy praise,
And be my salvation.

Longing

With sick and famished eyes,
With doubling knees and weary bones,
To thee my cries,
To thee my groans,
To thee my sighs, my tears ascend:
No end?

My throat, my soul is hoarse;
My heart is withered like a ground
Which thou dost curse.
My thoughts turn round,   10
And make me giddy; Lord, I fall,
Yet call.

From thee all pity flows.
Mothers are kind, because thou art,
And dost dispose
To them a part:
Their infants, them; and they suck thee
More free.

Bowels of pity, hear!
Lord of my soul, love of my mind,   20
Bow down thine ear!
Let not the wind
Scatter my words, and in the same
Thy name!

Look on my sorrow's round!
Mark well my furnace! O what flames,
What heats abound!
What griefs, what shames!
Consider, Lord; Lord, bow thine ear,
And hear!   30

Lord Jesu, thou didst bow
Thy dying head upon the tree:
O be not now
More dead to me!
Lord hear! *Shall he that made the ear,
Not hear?*

Behold, thy dust doth stir,
It moves, it creeps, it aims at thee:
Wilt thou defer
To succour me,
Thy pile of dust, wherein each crumb   40
Says, Come?

To thee help appertains.
Hast thou left all things to their course,
And laid the reins
Upon the horse?
Is all locked? hath a sinner's plea
No key?

Indeed the world's thy book,
Where all things have their leaf assigned: 50
Yet a meek look
Hath interlined.
Thy board is full, yet humble guests
Find nests.

Thou tarriest, while I die,
And fall to nothing: thou dost reign,
And rule on high,
While I remain
In bitter grief: yet am I styled
Thy child.   60

> Lord, didst thou leave thy throne,
> Not to relieve? how can it be,
> That thou art grown
> Thus hard to me?
> Were sin alive, good cause there were
> To bear.

> But now both sin is dead,
> And all thy promises live and bide.
> That wants his head;
> These speak and chide,   70
> And in thy bosom pour my tears,
> As theirs.

> Lord JESU, hear my heart,
> Which hath been broken now so long,
> That ev'ry part
> Hath got a tongue!
> Thy beggars grow; rid them away
> Today.

> My love, my sweetness, hear!
> By these thy feet, at which my heart   80
> Lies all the year,
> Pluck out thy dart,
> And heal my troubled breast which cries,
> Which dies.

The Bag

> Away despair! my gracious Lord doth hear.
> Though winds and waves assault my keel,
> He doth preserve it: he doth steer,
> Ev'n when the boat seems most to reel.
> Storms are the triumph of his art:
> Well may he close his eyes, but not his heart.

Hast thou not heard, that my Lord Jesus died?
    Then let me tell thee a strange story.
    The God of power, as he did ride
    In his majestic robes of glory,
    Resolved to light; and so one day   10
He did descend, undressing all the way.

The stars his tire of light and rings obtained,
    The cloud his bow, the fire his spear,
    The sky his azure mantle gained.
    And when they asked, what he would wear,
    He smiled and said as he did go,
He had new clothes a-making here below.

When he was come, as travellers are wont,
    He did repair unto an inn.   20
    Both then, and after, many a brunt
    He did endure to cancel sin:
    And having giv'n the rest before,
Here he gave up his life to pay our score.

But as he was returning, there came one
    That ran upon him with a spear.
    He, who came hither all alone,
    Bringing nor man, nor arms, nor fear,
    Received the blow upon his side,
And straight he turned, and to his brethren cried,   30

If ye have anything to send or write,
    I have no bag, but here is room:
    Unto my Father's hands and sight,
    Believe me, it shall safely come.
    That I shall mind, what you impart,
Look, you may put it very near my heart.

Or if hereafter any of my friends
    Will use me in this kind, the door
    Shall still be open; what he sends
    I will present, and somewhat more,   40
    Not to his hurt. Sighs will convey
Anything to me. Hark, Despair away.

The Jews

Poor nation, whose sweet sap and juice
Our scions have purloined, and left you dry:
Whose streams we got by the Apostles' sluice,
And use in baptism, while ye pine and die:
Who by not keeping once, became a debtor;
    And now by keeping lose the letter:

Oh that my prayers! mine, alas!
Oh that some angel might a trumpet sound;
At which the Church falling upon her face
Should cry so loud, until the trump were drowned,   10
And by that cry of her dear Lord obtain,
    That your sweet sap might come again!

The Collar

I struck the board, and cried, No more.
    I will abroad.
What? shall I ever sigh and pine?
My lines and life are free; free as the road,
    Loose as the wind, as large as store.
        Shall I be still in suit?
Have I no harvest but a thorn
To let me blood, and not restore
What I have lost with cordial fruit?
        Sure there was wine   10
Before my sighs did dry it: there was corn
    Before my tears did drown it.
    Is the year only lost to me?
        Have I no bays to crown it?
No flowers, no garlands gay? all blasted?
        All wasted?
Not so, my heart: but there is fruit,
    And thou hast hands.
Recover all thy sigh-blown age
On double pleasures: leave thy cold dispute   20

Of what is fit, and not. Forsake thy cage,
                    Thy rope of sands,
Which petty thoughts have made, and made to thee
                Good cable, to enforce and draw,
                        And be thy law,
            While thou didst wink and wouldst not see.
                    Away, Take Heed,
                    I will abroad,
Call in thy death's head there: tie up thy fears.
                    He that forbears   30
                    To suit and serve his need,
                        Deserves his load.
But as I raved and grew more fierce and wild
                    At every word,
Me thoughts I heard one calling, *Child!*
                    And I replied, *My Lord.*

The Glimpse

            Whither away delight?
Thou cam'st but now; wilt thou so soon depart,
            And give me up to night?
For many weeks of ling'ring pain and smart
But one half hour of comfort to my heart?

            Me thinks delight should have
More skill in music, and keep better time.
            Wert thou a wind or wave,
They quickly go and come with lesser crime:
Flowers look about, and die not in their prime.   10

            Thy short abode and stay
Feeds not, but adds to the desire of meat.
            Lime begged of old, they say,
A neighbour spring to cool his inward heat;
Which by the spring's access grew much more great.

In hope of thee my heart
Picked here and there a crumb, and would not die;
    But constant to his part,
Whenas my fears foretold this, did reply,
A slender thread a gentle guest will tie.   20

    Yet if the heart that wept
Must let thee go, return when it doth knock.
    Although thy heap be kept
For future times, the droppings of the stock
May oft break forth, and never break the lock.

    If I have more to spin,
The wheel shall go, so that thy stay be short.
    Thou know'st how grief and sin
Disturb the work. O make me not their sport,
Who by thy coming may be made a court!   30

Assurance

    O spiteful bitter thought!
Bitterly spiteful thought! Couldst thou invent
So high a torture? Is such poison bought?
Doubtless, but in the way of punishment.
        When wit contrives to meet with thee,
        No such rank poison can there be.

    Thou said'st but even now,
That all was not so fair, as I conceived,
Betwixt my God and me; that I allow
And coin large hopes, but that I was deceived: 10
        Either the league was broke, or near it;
        And, that I had great cause to fear it.

    And what to this? what more
Could poison, if it had a tongue, express?
What is thy aim? wouldst thou unlock the door
To cold despairs, and gnawing pensiveness?
        Wouldst thou raise devils? I see, I know,
        I writ thy purpose long ago.

But I will to my Father,
Who heard thee say it. O most gracious Lord,   20
If all the hope and comfort that I gather,
Were from myself, I had not half a word,
     Not half a letter to oppose
     What is objected by my foes.

But thou art my desert:
And in this league, which now my foes invade,
Thou art not only to perform thy part,
But also mine; as when the league was made
     Thou didst at once thyself indite,
     And hold my hand, while I did write.   30

Wherefore if thou canst fail,
Then can thy truth and I: but while rocks stand,
And rivers stir, thou canst not shrink or quail:
Yea, when both rocks and all things shall disband,
     Then shalt thou be my rock and tower,
     And make their ruin praise thy power.

Now foolish thought go on,
Spin out thy thread, and make thereof a coat
To hide thy shame: for thou hast cast a bone
Which bounds on thee, and will not down thy throat: 40
     What for itself love once began,
     Now love and truth will end in man.

The Call

Come, my Way, my Truth, my Life:
Such a Way, as gives us breath:
Such a Truth, as ends all strife:
Such a Life, as killeth death.

Come, my Light, my Feast, my Strength:
Such a Light, as shows a feast:
Such a Feast, as mends in length:
Such a Strength, as makes his guest.

Come, my Joy, my Love, my Heart:
Such a Joy, as none can move: 10
Such a Love, as none can part:
Such a Heart, as joys in love.

Clasping of Hands

Lord, thou art mine, and I am thine,
If mine I am: and thine much more,
Than I or ought, or can be mine.
Yet to be thine, doth me restore;
So that again I now am mine,
And with advantage mine the more,
Since this being mine, brings with it thine,
And thou with me dost thee restore.
    If I without thee would be mine,
    I neither should be mine nor thine.   10

Lord, I am thine, and thou art mine:
So mine thou art, that something more
I may presume thee mine, than thine.
For thou didst suffer to restore
Not thee, but me, and to be mine,
And with advantage mine the more,
Since thou in death wast none of thine,
Yet then as mine didst me restore.
    O be mine still! still make me thine!
    Or rather make no Thine and Mine!   20

Praise (III)

Lord, I will mean and speak thy praise,
        Thy praise alone.
My busy heart shall spin it all my days:
        And when it stops for want of store,
Then will I wring it with a sigh or groan,
        That thou mayst yet have more.

When thou dost favour any action,
      It runs, it flies:
All things concur to give it a perfection.
    That which had but two legs before,   10
When thou dost bless, hath twelve: one wheel doth rise
      To twenty then, or more.

    But when thou dost on business blow,
        It hangs, it clogs:
Not all the teams of Albion in a row
    Can hale or draw it out of door.
Legs are but stumps, and Pharaoh's wheels but logs,
      And struggling hinders more.

Thousands of things do thee employ
        In ruling all   20
This spacious globe: angels must have their joy,
    Devils their rod, the sea his shore,
The winds their stint: and yet when I did call,
      Thou heardst my call, and more.

I have not lost one single tear:
        But when mine eyes
Did weep to heav'n, they found a bottle there
    (As we have boxes for the poor)
Ready to take them in; yet of a size
      That would contain much more.   30

But after thou hadst slipped a drop
        From thy right eye,
(Which there did hang like streamers near the top
    Of some fair church, to show the sore
And bloody battle which thou once didst try)
      The glass was full and more.

Wherefore I sing. Yet since my heart,
        Though pressed, runs thin;
O that I might some other hearts convert,
    And so take up at use good store: 40
That to thy chest there might be coming in
      Both all my praise, and more!

Joseph's Coat

Wounded I sing, tormented I indite,
Thrown down I fall into a bed, and rest:
Sorrow hath changed its note: such is his will,
Who changeth all things, as him pleaseth best.
    For well he knows, if but one grief and smart
Among my many had his full career,
Sure it would carry with it ev'n my heart,
And both would run until they found a bier
    To fetch the body; both being due to grief.
But he hath spoiled the race; and giv'n to anguish   10
One of Joy's coats, ticing it with relief
To linger in me, and together languish.
    I live to show his power, who once did bring
    My *joys* to *weep*, and now my *griefs* to *sing*.

The Pulley

    When God at first made man,
Having a glass of blessings standing by;
Let us (said he) pour on him all we can:
Let the world's riches, which dispersèd lie,
    Contract into a span.

    So strength first made a way;
Then beauty flowed, then wisdom, honour, pleasure:
When almost all was out, God made a stay,
Perceiving that alone of all his treasure
    Rest in the bottom lay.   10

    For if I should (said he)
Bestow this jewel also on my creature,
He would adore my gifts instead of me,
And rest in Nature, not the God of Nature:
    So both should losers be.

Yet let him keep the rest,
But keep them with repining restlessness:
Let him be rich and weary, that at least,
If goodness lead him not, yet weariness
May toss him to my breast.   20

The Priesthood

Blest Order, which in power dost so excel,
That with th' one hand thou liftest to the sky,
And with the other throwest down to hell
In thy just censures; fain would I draw nigh,
Fain put thee on, exchanging my lay-sword
          For that of th' holy Word.

But thou art fire, sacred and hallowed fire;
And I but earth and clay: should I presume
To wear thy habit, the severe attire
My slender compositions might consume.   10
I am both foul and brittle; much unfit
          To deal in holy Writ.

Yet have I often seen, by cunning hand
And force of fire, what curious things are made
Of wretched earth. Where once I scorned to stand,
That earth is fitted by the fire and trade
Of skilful artists, for the boards of those
          Who make the bravest shows.

But since those great ones, be they ne'er so great,
Come from the earth, from whence those vessels come;   20
So that at once both feeder, dish, and meat
Have one beginning and one final sum:
I do not greatly wonder at the sight,
          If earth in earth delight.

But th' holy men of God such vessels are,
As serve him up, who all the world commands:
When God vouchsafeth to become our fare,

Their hands convey him, who conveys their hands.
O what pure things, most pure must those things be,
          Who bring my God to me!   30

Wherefore I dare not, I, put forth my hand
To hold the Ark, although it seem to shake
Through th' old sins and new doctrines of our land.
Only, since God doth often vessels make
Of lowly matter for high uses meet,
          I throw me at his feet.

There will I lie, until my Maker seek
For some mean stuff whereon to show his skill:
Then is my time. The distance of the meek
Doth flatter power. Lest good come short of ill   40
In praising might, the poor do by submission
          What pride by opposition.

The Search

Whither, O, whither art thou fled,
          My Lord, my Love?
My searches are my daily bread;
          Yet never prove.

My knees pierce th' earth, mine eyes the sky;
          And yet the sphere
And centre both to me deny
          That thou art there.

Yet can I mark how herbs below
          Grow green and gay,   10
As if to meet thee they did know,
          While I decay.

Yet can I mark how stars above
          Simper and shine,
As having keys unto thy love,
          While poor I pine.

I sent a sigh to seek thee out,
   Deep drawn in pain,
Winged like an arrow: but my scout
   Returns in vain.   20

I tuned another (having store)
   Into a groan;
Because the search was dumb before:
   But all was one.

Lord, dost thou some new fabric mould,
   Which favour wins,
And keeps thee present, leaving th' old
   Unto their sins?

Where is my God? what hidden place
   Conceals thee still?
What covert dare eclipse thy face? 30
   Is it thy will?

O let not that of anything;
   Let rather brass,
Or steel, or mountains be thy ring,
   And I will pass.

Thy will such an entrenching is,
   As passeth thought:
To it all strength, all subtilties
   Are things of nought.   40

Thy will such a strange distance is,
   As that to it
East and West touch, the poles do kiss,
   And parallels meet.

Since then my grief must be as large,
   As is thy space,
Thy distance from me; see my charge,
   Lord, see my case.

O take these bars, these lengths away;
                    Turn, and restore me: 50
Be not Almighty, let me say,
                    Against, but for me.

When thou dost turn, and wilt be near;
                    What edge so keen,
What point so piercing can appear
                    To come between?

For as thy absence doth excel
                    All distance known:
So doth thy nearness bear the bell,
                    Making two one.   60

Grief

O who will give me tears? Come all ye springs,
Dwell in my head and eyes: come clouds, and rain:
My grief hath need of all the wat'ry things,
That nature hath produced. Let ev'ry vein
Suck up a river to supply mine eyes,
My weary weeping eyes, too dry for me,
Unless they get new conduits, new supplies
To bear them out, and with my state agree.
What are two shallow fords, two little spouts
Of a less world? The greater is but small,   10
A narrow cupboard for my griefs and doubts,
Which want provision in the midst of all.
Verses, ye are too fine a thing, too wise
For my rough sorrows: cease, be dumb and mute,
Give up your feet and running to mine eyes,
And keep your measures for some lover's lute,
Whose grief allows him music and a rhyme:
For mine excludes both measure, tune, and time.
                    Alas, my God!

The Cross

What is this strange and uncouth thing?
To make me sigh, and seek, and faint, and die,
Until I had some place, where I might sing,
　　And serve thee; and not only I,
But all my wealth and family might combine
To set thy honour up, as our design.

　　And then when after much delay,
Much wrastling, many a combat, this dear end,
So much desired, is giv'n, to take away
　　My power to serve thee; to unbend
All my abilities, my designs confound,
And lay my threat'nings bleeding on the ground.

　　One ague dwelleth in my bones,
Another in my soul (the memory
What I would do for thee, if once my groans
　　Could be allowed for harmony):
I am in all a weak disabled thing,
Save in the sight thereof, where strength doth sting.

　　Besides, things sort not to my will,
Ev'n when my will doth study thy renown:
Thou turnest th' edge of all things on me still,
　　Taking me up to throw me down:
So that, ev'n when my hopes seem to be sped,
I am to grief alive, to them as dead.

　　To have my aim, and yet to be
Further from it than when I bent my bow;
To make my hopes my torture, and the fee
　　Of all my woes another woe,
Is in the midst of delicates to need,
And ev'n in Paradise to be a weed.

　　Ah my dear Father, ease my smart!
These contrarieties crush me: these cross actions
Do wind a rope about, and cut my heart:
　　And yet since these thy contradictions
Are properly a cross felt by thy Son,
With but four words, my words, *Thy will be done*.

The Flower

How fresh, O Lord, how sweet and clean
Are thy returns! ev'n as the flowers in spring;
 To which, besides their own demean,
The late-past frosts tributes of pleasure bring.
   Grief melts away
   Like snow in May,
As if there were no such cold thing.

Who would have thought my shrivelled heart
Could have recovered greenness? It was gone
 Quite under ground; as flowers depart
To see their mother-root, when they have blown;
   Where they together
   All the hard weather,
Dead to the world, keep house unknown.

These are thy wonders, Lord of power,
Killing and quick'ning, bringing down to hell
 And up to heaven in an hour;
Making a chiming of a passing-bell.
   We say amiss,
   This or that is:
Thy word is all, if we could spell.

O that I once past changing were,
Fast in thy Paradise, where no flower can wither!
 Many a spring I shoot up fair,
Off'ring at heav'n, growing and groaning thither:
   Nor doth my flower
   Want a spring-shower,
My sins and I joining together.

But while I grow in a straight line,
Still upwards bent, as if heav'n were mine own,
 Thy anger comes, and I decline:
What frost to that? what pole is not the zone,
   Where all things burn,
   When thou dost turn,
And the least frown of thine is shown?

And now in age I bud again,
After so many deaths I live and write;
    I once more smell the dew and rain,
And relish versing: O my only light,
                It cannot be   ·40
                That I am he
    On whom thy tempests fell all night.

    These are thy wonders, Lord of love,
To make us see we are but flowers that glide:
    Which when we once can find and prove,
Thou hast a garden for us, where to bide.
                Who would be more,
                Swelling through store,
    Forfeit their Paradise by their pride.

Dotage

False glozing pleasures, casks of happiness,
Foolish night-fires, women's and children's wishes,
Chases in arras, gilded emptiness,
Shadows well mounted, dreams in a career,
Embroidered lies, nothing between two dishes;
                These are the pleasures here.

True earnest sorrows, rooted miseries,
Anguish in grain, vexations ripe and blown,
Sure-footed griefs, solid calamities,
Plain demonstrations, evident and clear,   10
Fetching their proofs ev'n from the very bone;
                These are the sorrows here.

But oh the folly of distracted men,
Who griefs in earnest, joys in jest pursue;
Preferring, like brute beasts, a loathsome den
Before a court, ev'n that above so clear,
Where are no sorrows, but delights more true
                Than miseries are here!

The Son

Let foreign nations of their language boast,
What fine variety each tongue affords:
I like our language, as our men and coast:
Who cannot dress it well, want wit, not words.
How neatly do we give one only name
To parents' issue and the sun's bright star!
A son is light and fruit; a fruitful flame
Chasing the father's dimness, carried far
From the first man in th' East, to fresh and new
Western discov'ries of posterity.   10
So in one word our Lord's humility
We turn upon him in a sense most true:
    For what Christ once in humbleness began,
    We him in glory call, *The Son of Man*.

A True Hymn

My joy, my life, my crown!
My heart was meaning all the day,
    Somewhat it fain would say:
And still it runneth mutt'ring up and down
With only this, *My joy, my life, my crown*.

Yet slight not these few words:
If truly said, they may take part
    Among the best in art.
The fineness which a hymn or psalm affords,
Is, when the soul unto the lines accords.   10

He who craves all the mind,
And all the soul, and strength, and time,
    If the words only rhyme,
Justly complains, that somewhat is behind
To make his verse, or write a hymn in kind.

Whereas if th' heart be moved,
Although the verse be somewhat scant,
        God doth supply the want.
As when th' heart says (sighing to be approved)
O, could I love! and stops: God writeth, *Loved*.   20

The Answer

My comforts drop and melt away like snow:
I shake my head, and all the thoughts and ends,
Which my fierce youth did bandy, fall and flow
Like leaves about me: or like summer friends,
Flies of estates and sunshine. But to all,
Who think me eager, hot, and undertaking,
But in my prosecutions slack and small;
As a young exhalation, newly waking,
Scorns his first bed of dirt, and means the sky;
But cooling by the way, grows pursy and slow,   10
And settling to a cloud, doth live and die
In that dark state of tears: to all, that so
        Show me, and set me, I have one reply,
        Which they that know the rest, know more than I.

A Dialogue-Anthem

Christian. Death.

Chr. Alas, poor Death, where is thy glory?
        Where is thy famous force, thy ancient sting?
Dea. *Alas poor mortal, void of story,*
        Go spell and read how I have killed thy King.
Chr. Poor Death! and who was hurt thereby?
        Thy curse being laid on him, makes thee accurst.
Dea. *Let losers talk: yet thou shalt die;*
        These arms shall crush thee.
Chr.   Spare not, do thy worst.
        I shall be one day better than before:
        Thou so much worse, that thou shalt be no more.   10

The Water-course

Thou who dost dwell and linger here below,
Since the condition of this world is frail,
Where of all plants afflictions soonest grow;
If troubles overtake thee, do not wail:

For who can look for less, that loveth $\left\{\begin{array}{l} \text{Life?} \\ \text{Strife?} \end{array}\right.$

But rather turn the pipe and water's course
To serve thy sins, and furnish thee with store
Of sov'reign tears, springing from true remorse:
That so in pureness thou mayst him adore,

Who gives to man, as he sees fit, $\left\{\begin{array}{l} \text{Salvation.} \\ \text{Damnation.} \end{array}\right.$ 10

Self-condemnation

Thou who condemnest Jewish hate,
For choosing Barrabas a murderer
    Before the Lord of glory;
Look back upon thine own estate,
Call home thine eye (that busy wanderer):
    That choice may be thy story.

He that doth love, and love amiss,
This world's delights before true Christian joy,
    Hath made a Jewish choice:
The world an ancient murderer is;   10
Thousands of souls it hath and doth destroy
    With her enchanting voice.

He that hath made a sorry wedding
Between his soul and gold, and hath preferred
    False gain before the true,
Hath done what he condemns in reading:
For he hath sold for money his dear Lord,
    And is a Judas-Jew.

Thus we prevent the last great day,
And judge ourselves. That light, which sin and passion   20
    Did before dim and choke,
When once those snuffs are ta'en away,
Shines bright and clear, ev'n unto condemnation,
    Without excuse or cloak.

Bitter-sweet

Ah my dear angry Lord,
Since thou dost love, yet strike;
Cast down, yet help afford;
Sure I will do the like.

I will complain, yet praise;
I will bewail, approve:
And all my sour-sweet days
I will lament, and love.

The Glance

When first thy sweet and gracious eye
Vouchsafed ev'n in the midst of youth and night
To look upon me, who before did lie
    Welt'ring in sin;
I felt a sugared strange delight,
Passing all cordials made by any art,
Bedew, embalm, and overrun my heart,
    And take it in.

Since that time many a bitter storm
My soul hath felt, ev'n able to destroy,   10
Had the malicious and ill-meaning harm
    His swing and sway:
But still thy sweet original joy,
Sprung from thine eye, did work within my soul,
And surging griefs, when they grew bold, control,
    And got the day.

If thy first glance so powerful be,
A mirth but opened and sealed up again;
What wonders shall we feel, when we shall see
       Thy full-eyed love!   20
When thou shalt look us out of pain,
And one aspect of thine spend in delight
More than a thousand suns disburse in light,
       In heav'n above.

The 23d Psalm

The God of love my shepherd is,
       And he that doth me feed:
While he is mine, and I am his,
       What can I want or need?

He leads me to the tender grass,
       Where I both feed and rest;
Then to the streams that gently pass:
       In both I have the best.

Or if I stray, he doth convert
       And bring my mind in frame: 10
And all this not for my desert,
       But for his holy name.

Yea, in death's shady black abode
       Well may I walk, not fear:
For thou art with me; and thy rod
       To guide, thy staff to bear.

Nay, thou dost make me sit and dine,
       Ev'n in my enemies' sight:
My head with oil, my cup with wine
       Runs over day and night.   20

Surely thy sweet and wondrous love
       Shall measure all my days;
And as it never shall remove,
       So neither shall thy praise.

Mary Magdalene

When blessed Mary wiped her Saviour's feet,
(Whose precepts she had trampled on before)
And wore them for a jewel on her head,
    Showing his steps should be the street,
    Wherein she thenceforth evermore
With pensive humbleness would live and tread:

She being stained herself, why did she strive
To make him clean, who could not be defiled?
Why kept she not her tears for her own faults,
    And not his feet? Though we could dive   10
    In tears like seas, our sins are piled
Deeper than they, in words, and works, and thoughts.

Dear soul, she knew who did vouchsafe and deign
To bear her filth; and that her sins did dash
Ev'n God himself: wherefore she was not loth,
    As she had brought wherewith to stain,
    So to bring in wherewith to wash:
And yet in washing one, she washèd both.

Aaron

    Holiness on the head,
      Light and perfections on the breast,
Harmonious bells below, raising the dead
      To lead them unto life and rest:
        Thus are true Aarons drest.

    Profaneness in my head,
      Defects and darkness in my breast,
A noise of passions ringing me for dead
      Unto a place where is no rest:
        Poor priest thus am I drest.   10

Only another head
I have, another heart and breast,
Another music, making live not dead,
Without whom I could have no rest:
In him I am well drest.

Christ is my only head,
My alone only heart and breast,
My only music, striking me ev'n dead;
That to the old man I may rest,
And be in him new drest.   20

So holy in my head,
Perfect and light in my dear breast,
My doctrine tuned by Christ, (who is not dead,
But lives in me while I do rest)
Come people; Aaron's drest.

The Odour. 2. Cor. 2. 15

How sweetly doth *My Master* sound! *My Master*!
As ambergris leaves a rich scent
Unto the taster:
So do these words a sweet content,
An oriental fragrancy, *My Master*.

With these all day I do perfume my mind,
My mind ev'n thrust into them both:
That I might find
What cordials make this curious broth,
This broth of smells, that feeds and fats my mind.   10

My Master, shall I speak? O that to thee
My servant were a little so,
As flesh may be;
That these two words might creep and grow
To some degree of spiciness to thee!

Then should the pomander, which was before
   A speaking sweet, mend by reflection,
      And tell me more:
   For pardon of my imperfection
Would warm and work it sweeter than before. 20

For when *My Master*, which alone is sweet,
   And ev'n in my unworthiness pleasing,
      Shall call and meet,
   My servant, as thee not displeasing,
That call is but the breathing of the sweet.

This breathing would with gains by sweet'ning me
   (As sweet things traffic when they meet)
      Return to thee.
   And so this new commerce and sweet
Should all my life employ and busy me. 30

The Foil

    If we could see below
The sphere of virtue, and each shining grace
   As plainly as that above doth show;
This were the better sky, the brighter place.

    God hath made stars the foil
To set off virtues; griefs to set off sinning:
   Yet in this wretched world we toil,
As if grief were not foul, nor virtue winning.

The Forerunners

The harbingers are come. See, see their mark;
White is their colour, and behold my head.
But must they have my brain? must they dispark
Those sparkling notions, which therein were bred?
   Must dullness turn me to a clod?
Yet have they left me, *Thou art still my God.*

Good men ye be, to leave me my best room,
Ev'n all my heart, and what is lodgèd there:
I pass not, I, what of the rest become,
So *Thou art still my God*, be out of fear.   10
        He will be pleasèd with that ditty;
And if I please him, I write fine and witty.

Farewell sweet phrases, lovely metaphors.
But will ye leave me thus? when ye before
Of stews and brothels only knew the doors,
Then did I wash you with my tears, and more,
        Brought you to Church well dressed and clad:
My God must have my best, ev'n all I had.

Lovely enchanting language, sugar-cane,
Honey of roses, whither wilt thou fly?   20
Hath some fond lover ticed thee to thy bane?
And wilt thou leave the Church, and love a sty?
        Fie, thou wilt soil thy broidered coat,
And hurt thyself, and him that sings the note.

Let foolish lovers, if they will love dung,
With canvas, not with arras, clothe their shame:
Let folly speak in her own native tongue.
True beauty dwells on high: ours is a flame
        But borrowed thence to light us thither.
Beauty and beauteous words should go together.   30

Yet if you go, I pass not; take your way:
For, *Thou art still my God*, is all that ye
Perhaps with more embellishment can say.
Go birds of spring: let winter have his fee;
        Let a bleak paleness chalk the door,
So all within be livelier than before.

The Rose

Press me not to take more pleasure
        In this world of sugared lies,
And to use a larger measure
        Than my strict, yet welcome size.

First, there is no pleasure here:
       Coloured griefs indeed there are,
Blushing woes, that look as clear
       As if they could beauty spare.

Or if such deceits there be,
       Such delights I meant to say;   10
There are no such things to me,
       Who have passed my right away.

But I will not much oppose
       Unto what you now advise:
Only take this gentle rose,
       And therein my answer lies.

What is fairer than a rose?
       What is sweeter? yet it purgeth.
Purgings enmity disclose,
       Enmity forbearance urgeth.   20

If then all that worldlings prize
       Be contracted to a rose;
Sweetly there indeed it lies,
       But it biteth in the close.

So this flower doth judge and sentence
       Worldly joys to be a scourge:
For they all produce repentance,
       And repentance is a purge.

But I health, not physic choose:
       Only though I you oppose,   30
Say that fairly I refuse,
       For my answer is a rose.

Discipline

Throw away thy rod,
Throw away thy wrath:
       O my God,
Take the gentle path.

For my heart's desire
Unto thine is bent:
   I aspire
To a full consent.

Not a word or look
I affect to own,   10
   But by book,
And thy book alone.

Though I fail, I weep:
Though I halt in pace,
   Yet I creep
To the throne of grace.

Then let wrath remove;
Love will do the deed:
   For with love
Stony hearts will bleed.   20

Love is swift of foot;
Love's a man of war,
   And can shoot,
And can hit from far.

Who can scape his bow?
That which wrought on thee,
   Brought thee low,
Needs must work on me.

Throw away thy rod;
Though man frailties hath,   30
   Thou art God:
Throw away thy wrath.

The Invitation

Come ye hither All, whose taste
           Is your waste;
Save your cost, and mend your fare.
God is here prepared and dressed
           And the feast,
God, in whom all dainties are.

Come ye hither All, whom wine
           Doth define,
Naming you not to your good:
Weep what ye have drunk amiss,
           And drink this,   10
Which before ye drink is blood.

Come ye hither All, whom pain
           Doth arraign,
Bringing all your sins to sight:
Taste and fear not: God is here
           In this cheer,
And on sin doth cast the fright.

Come ye hither All, whom joy
           Doth destroy,   20
While ye graze without your bounds:
Here is joy that drowneth quite
           Your delight,
As a flood the lower grounds.

Come ye hither All, whose love
           Is your dove,
And exalts you to the sky:
Here is love, which having breath
           Ev'n in death,
After death can never die.   30

Lord I have invited all,
           And I shall
Still invite, still call to thee:

For it seems but just and right
                    In my sight,
Where is All, there All should be.

The Banquet

Welcome sweet and sacred cheer,
                    Welcome dear;
With me, in me, live and dwell:
For thy neatness passeth sight,
                    Thy delight
Passeth tongue to taste or tell.

O what sweetness from the bowl
                    Fills my soul,
Such as is, and makes divine!
Is some star (fled from the sphere)   10
                    Melted there,
As we sugar melt in wine?

Or hath sweetness in the bread
                    Made a head
To subdue the smell of sin;
Flowers, and gums, and powders giving
                    All their living,
Lest the Enemy should win?

Doubtless, neither star nor flower
                    Hath the power   20
Such a sweetness to impart:
Only God, who gives perfumes,
                    Flesh assumes,
And with it perfumes my heart.

But as pomanders and wood
                    Still are good,
Yet being bruised are better scented:
God, to show how far his love
                    Could improve,
Here, as broken, is presented.   30

When I had forgot my birth,
           And on earth
In delights of earth was drowned;
God took blood, and needs would be
           Spilt with me,
And so found me on the ground.

Having raised me to look up,
           In a cup
Sweetly he doth meet my taste.
But I still being low and short,   40
           Far from court,
Wine becomes a wing at last.

For with it alone I fly
           To the sky:
Where I wipe mine eyes, and see
What I seek, for what I sue;
           Him I view,
Who hath done so much for me.

Let the wonder of his pity
           Be my ditty,   50
And take up my lines and life:
Hearken under pain of death,
           Hands and breath;
Strive in this, and love the strife.

The Posy

           Let wits contest,
And with their words and posies windows fill:
           Less than the least
Of all thy mercies, is my posy still.

           This on my ring,
This by my picture, in my book I write:
           Whether I sing,
Or say, or dictate, this is my delight.

        Invention rest,
Comparisons go play, wit use thy will: 10
        Less than the least
Of all God's mercies, is my posy still.

A Parody

        Soul's joy, when thou art gone,
                And I alone,
                Which cannot be,
Because thou dost abide with me,
        And I depend on thee;

        Yet when thou dost suppress
                The cheerfulness
                Of thy abode,
And in my powers not stir abroad,
        But leave me to my load: 10

        O what a damp and shade
                Doth me invade!
                No stormy night
Can so afflict or so affright,
        As thy eclipsèd light.

        Ah Lord! do not withdraw,
                Lest want of awe
                Make Sin appear;
And when thou dost but shine less clear,
        Say, that thou art not here.   20

        And then what life I have,
                While Sin doth rave,
                And falsely boast,
That I may seek, but thou art lost;
        Thou and alone thou know'st.

        O what a deadly cold
                Doth me infold!
                I half believe,
That Sin says true: but while I grieve,
        Thou com'st and dost relieve.   30

The Elixir

Teach me, my God and King,
  In all things thee to see,
And what I do in anything,
  To do it as for thee:

Not rudely, as a beast,
  To run into an action;
But still to make thee prepossessed,
  And give it his perfection.

A man that looks on glass,
  On it may stay his eye;   10
Or if he pleaseth, through it pass,
  And then the heav'n espy.

All may of thee partake:
  Nothing can be so mean,
Which with his tincture (for thy sake)
  Will not grow bright and clean.

A servant with this clause
  Makes drudgery divine:
Who sweeps a room, as for thy laws,
  Makes that and th' action fine.   20

This is the famous stone
  That turneth all to gold:
For that which God doth touch and own
  Cannot for less be told.

A Wreath

A wreathèd garland of deservèd praise,
Of praise deservèd, unto thee I give,
I give to thee, who knowest all my ways,
My crooked winding ways, wherein I live,

Wherein I die, not live: for life is straight,
Straight as a line, and ever tends to thee,
To thee, who art more far above deceit,
Than deceit seems above simplicity.
Give me simplicity, that I may live,
So live and like, that I may know thy ways,   10
Know them and practise them: then shall I give
For this poor wreath, give thee a crown of praise.

Death

Death, thou wast once an uncouth hideous thing,
         Nothing but bones,
     The sad effect of sadder groans:
Thy mouth was open, but thou couldst not sing.

For we considered thee as at some six
         Or ten years hence,
     After the loss of life and sense,
Flesh being turned to dust, and bones to sticks.

We looked on this side of thee, shooting short;
         Where we did find   10
     The shells of fledge souls left behind,
Dry dust, which sheds no tears, but may extort.

But since our Saviour's death did put some blood
         Into thy face;
     Thou art grown fair and full of grace,
Much in request, much sought for as a good.

For we do now behold thee gay and glad,
         As at doomsday;
     When souls shall wear their new array,
And all thy bones with beauty shall be clad.   20

Therefore we can go die as sleep, and trust
         Half that we have
     Unto an honest faithful grave;
Making our pillows either down, or dust.

Doomsday

Come away,
Make no delay.
Summon all the dust to rise,
Till it stir, and rub the eyes;
While this member jogs the other,
Each one whisp'ring, *Live you brother?*

Come away,
Make this the day.
Dust, alas, no music feels,
But thy trumpet: then it kneels,   10
As peculiar notes and strains
Cure tarantula's raging pains.

Come away,
O make no stay!
Let the graves make their confession,
Lest at length they plead possession:
Flesh's stubbornness may have
Read that lesson to the grave.

Come away,
Thy flock doth stray.   20
Some to winds their body lend,
And in them may drown a friend:
Some in noisome vapours grow
To a plague and public woe.

Come away,
Help our decay.
Man is out of order hurled,
Parcelled out to all the world.
Lord, thy broken consort raise,
And the music shall be praise.   30

Judgement

Almighty Judge, how shall poor wretches brook
           Thy dreadful look,
Able a heart of iron to appal,
           When thou shalt call
    For ev'ry man's peculiar book?

What others mean to do, I know not well;
           Yet I hear tell,
That some will turn thee to some leaves therein
           So void of sin,
    That they in merit shall excel.   10

But I resolve, when thou shalt call for mine,
           That to decline,
And thrust a Testament into thy hand:
           Let that be scanned.
    There thou shalt find my faults are thine.

Heaven

O who will show me those delights on high?
         Echo.   I.
Thou Echo, thou art mortal, all men know.
         Echo.   No.
Wert thou not born among the trees and leaves?
         Echo.   Leaves.
And are there any leaves, that still abide?
         Echo.   Bide.
What leaves are they? impart the matter wholly.
         Echo.   Holy.   10
Are holy leaves the Echo then of bliss?
         Echo.   Yes.
Then tell me, what is that supreme delight?
         Echo.   Light.
Light to the mind: what shall the will enjoy?
         Echo.   Joy.

But are there cares and business with the pleasure?
    Echo. Leisure.
Light, joy, and leisure; but shall they persever?
    Echo. Ever.   20

Love (III)

Love bade me welcome: yet my soul drew back,
    Guilty of dust and sin.
But quick-eyed Love, observing me grow slack
    From my first entrance in,
Drew nearer to me, sweetly questioning,
    If I lacked anything.

A guest, I answered, worthy to be here:
    Love said, You shall be he.
I the unkind, ungrateful? Ah my dear,
    I cannot look on thee.   10
Love took my hand, and smiling did reply,
    Who made the eyes but I?

Truth Lord, but I have marred them: let my shame
    Go where it doth deserve.
And know you not, says Love, who bore the blame?
    My dear, then I will serve.
You must sit down, says Love, and taste my meat:
    So I did sit and eat.

FINIS

Glory be to God *on high*
And on earth peace
Goodwill towards men.

From Walton's *Life of Herbert*

Sonnets

My God, where is that ancient heat towards thee,
   Wherewith whole shoals of Martyrs once did burn,
   Besides their other flames? Doth Poetry
Wear Venus' livery? only serve her turn?
Why are not sonnets made of thee? and lays
   Upon thine Altar burnt? Cannot thy love
   Heighten a spirit to sound out thy praise
As well as any she? Cannot thy Dove
Outstrip their Cupid easily in flight?
   Or, since thy ways are deep, and still the same,   10
   Will not a verse run smooth that bears thy name?
Why doth that fire, which by thy power and might
   Each breast does feel, no braver fuel choose
   Than that, which one day worms may chance refuse?

Sure, Lord, there is enough in thee to dry
   Oceans of ink; for, as the Deluge did
   Cover the earth, so doth thy Majesty:
Each cloud distills thy praise, and doth forbid
Poets to turn it to another use.
   Roses and lilies speak thee; and to make
   A pair of cheeks of them, is thy abuse.
Why should I women's eyes for crystal take?
Such poor invention burns in their low mind
   Whose fire is wild, and doth not upward go   10
   To praise, and on thee, Lord, some ink bestow.
Open the bones, and you shall nothing find
   In the best face but filth, when, Lord, in thee
   The beauty lies in the discovery.

Notes

ABBREVIATIONS

B	The Bodleian manuscript of Herbert's *Temple*
BCP	The Book of Common Prayer
Hutchinson	Herbert's *Works*, edited by F. E. Hutchinson
OED	*The Oxford English Dictionary*
W	The early manuscript of Herbert's poems, in Dr Williams's Library, Gordon Square, London.
Walton, *Life*	Izaak Walton, *The Life of Mr. George Herbert* (1670), in Walton, *Lives*, World's Classics edn. (London: Oxford University Press, 1927).
1633	The first edition of Herbert's *Temple*.

1 *The Dedication.* l. 6. *refrain*: stop, prevent.

2 *The Church-porch. Perirrhanterium*: instrument used for sprinkling holy water.

l. 15. *afford*: give, grant.

l. 16. *stays*: restraints.

ll. 19–20. *common . . . th' incloser.* The imagery is drawn from the practice of enclosing public grazing land (the 'common') for private use.

l. 21. *impaled*: fenced in.

l. 24. *cross*: perverse, contrary.

3 l. 27. *list*: desire, like, choose.

l. 30. *keep the round*: i.e. drink at each pass of the bottle.

l. 35. *devest*: annul, in legal usage; abandon.

l. 37. *wine-sprung*: drunk.

l. 39. *can*: drinking vessel. Hutchinson paraphrases 38–40, 'I may not drink what the hardened drinker allows himself; need I humour him to my own undoing?'

l. 44. *several*: separate.

l. 50. Phil. 3: 19, 'Whose end is destruction, whose God is their belly, and whose glory is in their shame, who mind earthly things.'

l. 53. *flat*: unconditional, outright.

4 l. 60. *Epicure*: a follower of the philosophy of Epicurus; 'one who recognizes no religious motives for conduct' (*OED*).   *bate*: omit.

l. 80. An echo of Donne's 'To Mr. Tilman': 'As if their day were only to be spent | In dressing, mistressing and compliment' (29–30).

l. 83. *brave*: splendid, grand.

5 l. 92. *phlegm*. The phlegmatic humour was thought to cause sloth when it was in preponderance over the other three humours (blood, black and yellow bile); thus the modern 'phlegmatic'.

l. 99. *mark*: note the place where the game bird has hidden after having been flushed out.   *fashion*: behaviour, but also with the sense of 'fashioning' or education.

l. 100. *ship them over*: i.e. send them abroad.

l. 102. Hutchinson paraphrases, 'If thou art not moved by thy child being in God's image (see l. 379 and Gen. 1: 26), be careful of him as being in thine own image.'

6 l. 117. *stour*: strong, stout.

l. 118. *thrall*: thraldom.

l. 120. Nature makes man a ship, but man makes himself into a reef ('shelf') on which he founders.

l. 124. *clue*: a ball of thread or yarn.

l. 128. *sconces*: forts, earthworks.

l. 132. *withal*: in addition. The second half of the line is a quotation from the Burial Office in the Book of Common Prayer.

l. 137. *ecliptic line*: orbit of the sun in the Ptolemaic system.

l. 142. *parcel*: part.   *underwrites*: confirms by signing.

7 l. 145. *use*: habitually practise.

l. 146. *Salute*: 'Greet with some gesture ... of respect or courteous recognition' (*OED*).

ll. 157–60. 'Youth can afford to spend all the year's income, but age must make provision for the declining years' (Hutchinson).

l. 169. *What skills it*: What does it matter, what good is it?

l. 171. *told*: counted. See Luke 12: 33, 'provide yourselves bags which wax not old, a treasure in the heavens that faileth not.'

8 l. 179. *curious*: fastidious, particular (about fashions).   *unthrift*: spendthrift.

l. 187. *bear the bell*: win first prize.

l. 190. *brave*: elegant, fine.

l. 191. *curiousness*: fastidiousness in dressing.

ll. 197–8. 'When a man's very name was passing out of local memory, a herald, making his official Visitation every thirty years or so, after some search ('at length') finds it in a cracked church-window' (Hutchinson).

l. 204. *increase*: profits, but also children.

9 l. 205. *conversation*: 'manner of conducting oneself in the world or in society' (*OED*).

l. 207. *assay*: try, attempt.

l. 208. *bravery*. Often used in the sense of 'an act of bravado'—swaggering; but this shades into the modern meaning, as in l. 222.

l. 211. *complexion*: temperament.

l. 212. *allay*: alloy.

l. 217. *Catch at*: snatch at; be eager to enter quarrels.

l. 218. *home*: 'to the point', 'close to the mark'.

l. 223. *posed*: questioned.

l. 227. *plays*: manages.

l. 228. *toy*: trivial thing.

l. 232. *conceit*: witticism. 'Conceit' is the object of 'advance'.

10 l. 240. *vein*: aptitude, disposition.

l. 244. *want*: lack.

l. 247. *sad*: serious, solemn.

l. 248. *van*: front-line of an attacking army.

l. 250. *fired beacon*: a warning of danger.   *ditties*: words for songs.

l. 252. *cock*: victor.

l. 253. *respective*: respectful.

l. 254. *temper*: disposition, temperament.

l. 256. *rateably*: proportionately.

l. 258. *parcel-devil*: part-devil, joint-devil.

11 ll. 265–6. *bate . . . honour*: diminish the honour due the place.

l. 272. *still*: always.

l. 276. *David . . . Jonathan*: see 1 Sam. 18.

ll. 287–8. 'Even love cannot make more than *one man* of me, and to attempt more would only make my inability run up a score against me' (Hutchinson).

12 l. 297. *rest*: in primero (a card game), the stakes held in reserve.

13 l. 327. *parts*: abilities, talents.   *great places*: high or important positions.

ll. 329–30: *go less | To*: fall short of.

l. 334. *means*: aims at.

l. 341. *spirits live alone*: such spirits alone truly live.

l. 348. *quit*: pay, pay off.

l. 352. *sling*. Alludes to story of David and Goliath, 1 Sam. 17.

14 l. 365. *fit*: activity, inclination.

l. 367. *Affect*: be drawn to, have affection for (cleanliness).

l. 368. *board*: come close to, approach.

15 l. 391. *Twice . . . understood.* It is our duty to attend service twice on Sunday.

l. 393. *cheer*: food; also comfort ('mended' by spiritual quality).
bate of: reduce the amount of.

l. 395. *cross*: perverse.

l. 396. *Fast . . . loss.* 'Fasting may be *gain* any day *but then*.' (Hutchinson)

l. 397. *brave*: excellent, splendid.

l. 401. *six and seven*: a phrase from gambling with dice, 'denoting the hazard of one's whole fortune, or carelessness as to the consequences of one's actions' (*OED*).

l. 403. *bare*: bare-headed.

l. 407. *quit thy state*: give up your high position or stately manner.

l. 409. *Resort to*: go to frequently.

16 l. 422. *plots*: plans, not necessarily evil ones.

l. 428. *conceiv'st him not*: do not understand him.

l. 429. *See* 1 Cor. 1: 21 'it pleased God by the foolishness of preaching to save them that believe.'

l. 430. See 2 Cor. 4: 7, 'But we have this treasure in earthen vessels.'

l. 443. *condition*: character, nature, state of being.

17 l. 449. *refusèd thunder*. Referring to the Law set forth with thunder on Mt. Sinai (Exod. 19: 16), and to 1 Cor. 1: 18, 'For the preaching of the cross is to them that perish foolishness.'

l. 450. See Job 3: 23, 'Why is light given to a man whose way is hid, and whom God hath hedged in?'

l. 460. *ell*: a unit of measure (45 inches).

Superliminare: lintel above the entrance.

l. 4. *mystical*: 'Having a certain spiritual character or import by virtue of a connexion or union with God . . . said esp. with reference to the Church as the Body of Christ, and to sacramental ordinances' (*OED*).

l. 5. *Avoid*. A command: 'withdraw'.

18 *The Church. The Altar.* A long tradition lies behind Herbert's use of the shaped poem (see also *Easter-wings*); notable examples may be found in the Greek Anthology.

ll. 1–2. *broken . . . heart.* See Ps. 51: 17, 'The sacrifices of God are a broken spirit: a broken and a contrite heart, O God, thou wilt not despise.'

l. 3. *frame*: form, shape.

l. 4. Exod. 20: 25, 'And if thou wilt make me an altar of stone, thou shalt not build it of hewn stone: for if thou lift up thy tool upon it, thou hast polluted it.'

l. 5. The poem implicitly alludes to 2 Cor. 3: 2–3, 'Ye are our epistle written in our hearts . . . Forasmuch as ye are manifestly declared to be the epistle of Christ ministered by us, written not with ink, but with the Spirit of the living God; not in tables of stone, but in fleshy tables of the heart.'

l. 11. *frame*: structure, including the body, this poem, and 'The Church'.

ll. 13–14. Luke 19: 40, 'I tell you that, if these [the disciples] should hold their peace, the stones would immediately cry out.'

The Sacrifice. Spoken by Christ from the Cross, in a tradition deriving from the medieval liturgy for Holy Week, especially the 'Reproaches' spoken on Good Friday. The poem coalesces the story of the Passion as recorded in Matt. 26–7, Mark 14–15, Luke 22–3, and John 18–19.

l. 1. See Lamentations 1: 12, 'Is it nothing to you, all ye that pass by? behold, and see if there be any sorrow like unto my sorrow.'

l. 4. *grief*: along with its modern meaning, in Herbert's day the word retained its older meaning of physical pain, bodily injury, wound.

l. 5. *make a head*: advance against.

l. 7. *except*: unless.

l. 9. *brave*: treat insolently.

19 l. 13. *apostle.* Judas, who was the treasurer for the disciples, 'had the bag' (John 12: 6).

l. 18. *at three hundred.* When Mary Magdalene anointed Christ's feet with oil, Judas said, 'Why was not this ointment sold for three hundred pence, and given to the poor?' (John 12: 5).

l. 22. *the only beads*: an allusion to counting beads while saying the rosary.

l. 23. The prayer of Jesus in Gethsemane: 'O my Father, if it be possible, let this cup pass from me: nevertheless not as I will, but as thou wilt' (Matt. 26: 39).

l. 25. *tempered*: mixed.

l. 38. *Way and Truth*. John 14: 6, 'I am the way, the truth, and the life.'

20 l. 47. *loosed their bands*. See Ezek. 34: 27, 'they shall be safe in their land, and shall know that I am the Lord, when I have broken the bands of their yoke.'   *bands*: anything that binds the limbs or body.

l. 59. *Paschal Lamb*: the lamb slain as Passover; a term traditionally applied to Christ.

l. 63. *any robbery*: Phil. 2: 6, 'Who, being in the form of God, thought it not robbery to be equal with God.'

ll. 65–6. See John 2: 19–21, where the words of Jesus are applied to 'the temple of his body'.

l. 71. Adam took his first breath from God, and now his descendants return the breath by condemning God.

21 l. 77. *set me light*: despise me.

l. 85. *despitefulness*: contemptuousness.

l. 89. *prove*: test, try.

ll. 94–5. A reference to the story of Noah's ark. See especially Gen. 8: 8–9.

l. 107. Matt. 27: 25, 'Then answered all the people, and said, His blood be on us, and on our children.'

22 l. 113. *a murderer*: Barabbas. See Matt. 27: 15–26.

ll. 118–19. *peace . . . understanding*. Phil. 4: 7, 'the peace of God, which passeth all understanding.'   *doth glass*: i.e. surpasses glass (see 1 Cor. 13: 12).

l. 122. This is spoken ironically. It was God, through Moses, who brought water from a rock (Exod. 17: 6, Num. 20: 11, Ps. 78: 16).

l. 127. *mysteriousness*: a 'mystery' in the theological sense: 'a doctrine of the faith involving difficulties which human reason is incapable of solving' (*OED*).

l. 129. *list*: wish.

l. 134. John 9: 6, 'he [Jesus] spat on the ground, and made clay of the spittle, and he anointed the eyes of the blind man with the clay.'

l. 138. Exod. 34: 33, 'till Moses had done speaking with them, he put a vail on his face.'

23 l. 141. *abjects*: outcast or degraded people.

l. 142. *ditty*: words (for a song or chant); see Matt. 26: 68; Luke 22: 64.

ll. 149–50. With allusion to Christ's bloody sweat in the garden of Gethsemane, Luke 22: 44.

ll. 161–3. for the imagery of this passage, see Isa. 5: 1–7.

ll. 165–7. Hutchinson paraphrases, 'The *curse in Adam's fall* brought thorns upon the earth (Gen. 3: 18), and now a crown of thorns is put *unto my brows.'*   *thrall*: thraldom, servitude.

l. 170. *my head, the rock.* 1 Cor. 10: 4, 'for they drank of that spiritual Rock that followed them: and that Rock was Christ.' This passage is a typological interpretation of the rock of Horeb (Exod. 17: 6). See the note to l. 122.

24 l. 175. *sink*: cesspool.

l. 178. *weeds*: clothing, but with a pun on the modern sense.

l. 185. *rout*: mob.

l. 193. *engross*: concentrate.

l. 199. *The decreed burden*: Matt. 16: 24, 'Then said Jesus unto his disciples, If any man will come after me, let him deny himself, and take up his cross, and follow me.'

l. 203. *but*: except.

25 ll. 205–7. 'The natural world came into being by mere divine Fiat, but *a world of sin* can only be redeemed at greater cost than by words' (Hutchinson).

ll. 213–15. See Matt. 27: 46; Mark 15: 34, 'My God, my God, why hast thou forsaken me?' The cry echoes Ps. 22: 1.

l. 221. See Luke 4: 23; Matt. 27: 40; Mark 15: 30.

l. 233. *prefixed on high.* With double meaning: first, with reference to the sign 'set up over his head', reading 'This is Jesus the King of the Jews' (Matt. 27: 37; Luke 23: 38); and secondly, with the implication that this fate was decreed 'on high' by God long beforehand.

26 l. 239. *manna*: see Exod. 16: 14–15. *Angels' food*: Ps. 78: 25, 'Man did eat angels' food.'

ll. 242–3. *My coat . . . help*: Matt. 14: 35–6, 'they sent out into all that country round about, and brought unto him all that were diseased; And besought him that they might only touch the hem of his garment: and as many as touched were made perfectly whole.'

l. 250. *weal*: welfare, happiness.

The Thanksgiving. l. 1. *grief.* See note on *The Sacrifice, l.* 4.

l. 4. *preventest*: comes before; also, surpasses.

ll. 5–6. With allusion to Christ in the garden of Gethsemane, Luke 22: 44, 'and his sweat was as it were great drops of blood falling down.'   *store*: abundance.

l. 9. See note on *The Sacrifice*, ll. 213–15.

l. 14. *posy*: a bouquet; also, a collection of poems.

l. 16. *hand*: handwriting.

27 l. 33. *spittle*: hospital; poorhouse.   *common ways*: public highways.

l. 43. *wit*: intelligence.

l. 47. *art of love*. With ironic allusion to Ovid's *Ars Amatoria*.

The Reprisal. The title includes the sense of 'reprise': a renewal of an action or theme previously attempted. In *W* this poem is entitled *The Second Thanksgiving*.

28 l. 6. *disentangled*: debt-free.

l. 8. *by thy death*. i.e. through the redemptive power of your death I have the strength to die for you.

The Agony. The title is the traditional name for the scene of Christ's anguish and bloody sweat in the garden of Gethsemane, or the Mount of Olives: Luke 22: 39–44; Matt. 26: 36–9.

l. 1. *Philosophers*: thinkers in all areas of 'philosophy', especially 'natural philosophy', science.

l. 3. *staff*: a surveyor's instrument for measuring heights and distances; also, a 'divining rod' for finding water.

l. 5. *doth more behove*: is more necessary.

l. 7. *repair*: go.

l. 11. *press*: the wine-press, traditional eucharistic image.

l. 13. *assay*: test the nature of.

29 *The Sinner*. l. 1. *ague*: an acute fever, especially a malarial fever.

l. 7. *cross*: perverse, contrary.

l. 11. *the many hundred part*: i.e. one part in many hundreds.

l. 14. *write in stone*: Exod. 31: 18, 'two tables of testimony, tables of stone, written with the finger of God.'

Good Friday. l. 4. *tell*: count up, reckon the value of; also, narrate.

ll. 11–12. *fruit . . . true vine*. John 15: 1–2, 'I am the true vine, and my Father is the husbandman. . . . and every branch that beareth fruit, he purgeth it, that it may bring forth more fruit.'

30 l. 18. *several*: individual.

Redemption. In *W* this poem is entitled *The Passion*.

l. 9. *straight*: straightway, immediately.

l. 10. *resorts*: places where people are accustomed to gather.

31 *Sepulchre*. l. 5. *good store*: in good measure.

l. 7. *toys*: trivialities.

l. 13. *took up stones*: John 10: 31, 'Then the Jews took up stones again to stone him.'

l. 18. *writ in stone*. See note on *The Sinner*, l. 14.

l. 19. *no fit heart*. See note on *The Altar*, l. 5.

32 *Easter*. l. 13. *Consort*: harmonize.   *twist*: interlace musical parts.

l. 15. *three parts*: the three tones of a chord.   *vied*: placed in competition.

ll. 19–30. *W* gives an earlier version of these lines as a separate poem entitled *Easter*. As printed, however, the lines make up the song promised in l. 13. *straw*: strew.

l. 22. *sweets*: fragrancies.

l. 29. *miss*: miscount; err.

33 *Easter-wings*. l. 1. *store*: abundance.

l. 10. This line refers to the 'fortunate fall', the view that Adam's fall was fortunate since it occasioned Christ's incarnation and man's redemption.

l. 19. *imp*: engraft an injured wing with feathers.

H. Baptism (I). l. 7. *prevent*: come before, anticipate (along with modern sense).

34 l. 13. *miscall*: misname, but also with the sense of 'malign' or 'abuse'.

H. Baptism (II) l. 2. *A narrow way and little gate*. Matt. 7: 14, 'strait is the gate, and narrow is the way, which leadeth unto life.'

l. 10. *behither*: short of, barring.

Nature. ll. 5–6. 2 Cor. 10: 4, 'For the weapons of our warfare are not carnal, but mighty through God to the pulling down of strong holds.'

l. 9. *straight*: immediately.

l. 10. *by kind*: according to nature.

35 ll. 13–14. Jer. 31: 33, 'I will put my law in their inward parts, and write it in their hearts.'

Sin (I). l. 6. *sorted*: assorted, varied.

l. 14. *bosom-sin*: a deeply cherished sin, close to the heart.

Affliction (I). l. 2. *brave*: splendid, elegant.

l. 7. *furniture*: furnishings.

36 l. 12. *mirth*: joy, happiness, pleasure.

l. 21. *strawed*: strewn.

l. 24. *party*: side in a contest.

l. 25. *began*: i.e. began to complain. The complaints of the flesh are recorded in the next three lines.

37 l. 47. *where.* The reading of *W*; *B* and *1633* have 'neere', although in *B* 'where' is written above it, apparently as a correction.

l. 53. *cross-bias*: give an inclination counter to. The metaphor is from the game of bowls; a 'bias' altered the course of the ball.

l. 60. *just*: 'Adapted to something else, or to an end or purpose; appropriate; suitable' (*OED*).

ll. 65–6. 'Although it may seem that I have been completely forgotten by you (or: although I have completely forgotten what I owe to you), I love you, and if I should not love you, I deserve the penalty of being denied the power of loving you.

Repentance. l. 3. *quick*: living, but also, briefly flowering.

38 l. 14. *compassionate*: a verb, to treat with compassion.

l. 21. *wormwood.* Jer. 9: 15, 'thus saith the Lord of hosts . . . Behold, I will feed them, even this people, with wormwood.'

l. 22. *stay*: delay, stay away.

ll. 25–6. Ps. 39: 11, 'When thou with rebukes dost correct man for iniquity, thou makest his beauty to consume away like a moth.'

l. 26. *waxeth*: becomes, turns.   *woe*: woeful, sorrowful.

l. 32. Ps. 51: 8, 'Make me to hear joy and gladness; that the bones which thou hast broken may rejoice.'

Faith. l. 6. *conceit*: imagine.

39 l. 9. *outlandish*: foreign.

l. 11. A reference to Gen. 3: 15, 'And I will put enmity between thee and the woman, and between thy seed and her seed; it shall bruise thy head, and thou shalt bruise his heel.'

l. 30. *clerk*: clergyman.

l. 35. *allow*: accept as.

l. 37. *clean*: entirely.

40 *Prayer* (I). l. 1. *banquet.* The modern meaning may be present, but in Herbert's day the word also indicated 'a course of sweetmeats, fruit, and wine, served either as a separate entertainment, or as a continuation of the principal meal' (*OED*). See *The Banquet*, where the title is closely associated with 'sweetness'.   *angels' age.* 'Prayer acquaints man with the blessed timeless existence of the angels' (Hutchinson).

l. 2. Gen. 2: 7, 'And the Lord God formed man of the dust of the ground, and breathed into his nostrils the breath of life.'

l. 3. *soul in paraphrase.* 'In prayer the soul opens out and more fully discovers itself' (Hutchinson).

l. 5. *Engine*: any machine used against fortifications, such as a battering-ram or catapult.

l. 7. *transposing*: putting into a different musical key (see 'tune' below); the *six-days' world* of the Creation may be regarded in musical terms as a hexachord.

l. 10. *manna*: see Exod. 16: 14–15.

l. 11. *in ordinary*. A common phrase indicating something that occurs 'in the ordinary course, as a regular custom or practice' (*OED*). An *ordinary* was also 'a regular daily meal', a meal provided at an eating-house, or the eating-house itself (*OED*); hence here a means or place of spiritual refreshment.

l. 12. *bird of Paradise*. In Herbert's day the bird was thought to live continually in the air, never touching the earth.

The H. Communion. W has only the second part of this poem (ll. 25–40), which it entitles *Prayer. W* contains a different poem called *The H. Communion*, not printed in *1633*.

ll. 1–2. For the story of the punishment of Achan, who coveted 'a goodly Babylonish garment' and 'a wedge of gold,' see Josh. 7: 19–26.
      furniture: furnishings.

l. 5. *without*: outside.

41 l. 13. *these*: the physical 'elements' of the service, the bread and wine.

l. 16. *outworks*: outer defences.

l. 21. *privy*: private, secret.

l. 23. *those*: the elements (l. 19), i.e. the bread and wine, changed into vapours ('spirits') rising from the blood.

l. 24. *friend*: Christ.

42 *Antiphon* (I). An antiphon is normally a hymn sung responsively by two choirs; here the abbreviation 'Vers.' indicates the 'versicle' spoken or sung by the priest or minister leading the service, after which the congregation responds as a chorus.

Love I. l. 1. *this great frame*: the universe.

l. 6. *invention*: inventiveness, creativity.

43 *Love* II. l. 6. *pant*: pant after.

l. 12. *disseized*: dispossessed.

l. 13. *All knees shall bow*. Isa. 45: 23, 'That unto me every knee shall bow.'

The Temper (I). The word 'temper' means 'the due or proportionate mixture of elements or qualities' (*OED*). While the primary meaning here and in the next poem refers to a well-proportioned soul, Herbert plays with the sense of 'tempering' steel to harden it, and with the sense of 'tempering' or tuning a musical instrument.

l. 5. *some forty*. This number seems arbitrarily chosen to indicate an indefinite large number.

l. 13. *meet*. With a pun on 'mete' (measure), referring to the measuring of swords before a duel (Hutchinson).

l. 16. *spell*: 'consider, contemplate, scan intently' (*OED*).

44 *The Temper* (II). l. 4. *that*: the 'mighty joy' of l. 1.

l. 7. *race*: raze.

l. 9. *chair of grace*. Perhaps a reference to the 'mercy seat' carried in the Ark of the Covenant (Exod. 25: 17) that Solomon 'fixed' in the Temple of Jerusalem (1 Chron. 28: 11). The mercy seat came to signify the throne of God in heaven.

45 *Jordan* (I). Since the Jordan was the river in which Christ was baptized, the primary implication seems to be the 'baptism' of Herbert's muse: the Jordan replaces the springs of the Muses on Mount Helicon as a source of poetic inspiration. At the same time the Jordan was regarded as dividing the Holy Land from the lands to the East: thus the title may also suggest a division between the sacred and the secular.

l. 5. *painted chair*. This phrase may suggest a reference to *Republic* x. i-viii, where Socrates, as part of his attack on 'mimetic poetry', argues that a painting of a couch is at two removes from reality, in that it imitates a couch, which itself imitates the 'idea' of a couch.

l. 7. *sudden arbours*: 'that appear unexpectedly, it being an aim of the designer of a garden that it should have surprises' (Hutchinson).
    shadow: provide shade for, but also, sketch or paint.

l. 12. *who list*: whoever wishes.   *pull for prime*: in the card game primero, 'to draw for a card or cards which will make the player *prime*' (*OED*), i.e. give him the winning hand.

Employment (I). l. 8. *doom*: Judgement Day.

46 l. 23. *consort*: a group of musicians.

l. 24. *reed*: a wood-wind instrument, but see also Isa. 42: 3, 'A bruised reed shall he not break.'

The H. Scriptures I. ll. 1–2. Ps. 119: 103, 'How sweet are thy words unto my taste! yea, sweeter than honey to my mouth!' Also, Ezek. 2: 9, 3: 3, 'and, lo, a roll of a book was therein ... Then did I eat it; and it was in my mouth as honey for sweetness.'

l. 8. *thankful*: worthy of thanks.

l. 11. *lidger*: ledger, or lieger: a resident ambassador.

l. 13. *handsel*: a token or gift implying good to come.

The H. Scriptures II. l. 2. *configurations*: the relative positions of the stars and planets.

47 l. 7. *watch a potion*: watch for opportunities to make up a medicine (with allusion to the current belief in a live relation between the stars and the growth of vegetation).

Whitsunday: the seventh Sunday after Easter, the festival of Pentecost, which commemorates the coming of the Holy Spirit to the Apostles. See Acts 2.

l. 17. *pipes of gold*. Zech. 4: 12, 14, 'What be these two olive branches which through the two golden pipes empty the golden oil out of themselves? ... These are the two anointed ones, that stand by the Lord of the whole earth.' Herbert thus represents the Apostles as the conduits of God's grace.

48 l. 23. *braves*: insolent challenges.

Grace. l. 1. *stock*: a tree-trunk with branches cut off, a stump. See Job 14: 7–8, 'For there is hope of a tree, if it be cut down, that it will sprout again ... Though the root thereof wax old in the earth, and the stock thereof die in the ground.' But the meaning of 'estate' or 'property' is also present.

49 *Praise* (I). l. 11. *sling*: a reference to the sling with which David killed Goliath (1 Sam. 17: 23–51).

ll. 13–16. The poor, who can ascend to God, may outstrip the 'herb', which ascends only to the head.

Affliction (II) l. 4. *broken pay*: payment by instalments.

l. 5. *Methusalem's stay*: Gen. 5: 27, 'And all the days of Methuselah were nine hundred sixty and nine years.'

l. 10. *discolour*: take the colour from.   *bloody sweat*. Another allusion to the Agony (see note on poem by that title).

50 l. 15. *imprest*: advance payment.

Mattens: matins, morning prayer.

51 *Sin* (II). ll. 4–5. Evil was commonly thought to lack real substance, to be only a privation of good.

l. 10. *in perspective*: as in a drawing or painting done according to principles of perspective (see 'paint', l. 2).

52 *Church-monuments*. The text here follows *B* and *W* in not dividing the poem into six-line stanzas, as implied by the rhyme-scheme and so divided in *1633*. The effect of 'death's incessant motion' may be enhanced by the way in which the poem's movement overrides the expected formal divisions. The intimate colloquy with the flesh is emphasized by the indentation of line 17 in *W*.

l. 8. *elements*: letters of the alphabet, with a pun on the material elements, earth, air, fire, and water.

l. 24. *fit thyself against*: prepare yourself for (death); also, prepare to meet the consequences of (the fall of man).

53 *Church-music.* l. 1. *Sweetest of sweets.* The phrase, together with 'sweetly' in l. 7, provides a striking example of Herbert's rich and varied uses of 'sweet' and its derivatives. Here 'sweets' means primarily 'pleasures', 'delights'. But the adjective 'sweet' could also mean 'pleasing to the ear; having or giving a pleasant sound; musical, melodious, harmonious: said of a sound, a voice, an instrument, a singer or performer on an instrument' (*OED*): thus church music is the sweetest of all music. Furthermore, l. 7, 'We both together sweetly live and love', brings in the connotations retained in 'sweetheart', with 'sweetly', implying a relationship of deep affection.

l. 9. *post*: hurry.

54 *The Church-floor.* l. 10. *one sure band.* Col. 3: 14, 'And above all these things put on charity, which is the bond of perfectness.'

l. 14. *curious*: fine, delicate.

The Windows. l. 2. *crazy*: full of flaws and cracks.

l. 6. *anneal in glass*: fix the painting on the glass by a process of heating.

55 *Trinity Sunday*: the Sunday following Whitsunday; that is, the eighth Sunday after Easter: a Sunday dedicated to the celebration of the Trinity.

56 *Content.* l. 15. *let loose to*: aim at (the image is from archery).

l. 28. *rent*: rend; i.e., be rent.

l. 33. *discoursing*: 'busily thinking, passing rapidly from one thought to another' (*OED*).

The Quiddity. In *W* this poem is entitled *Poetry.* A 'quiddity' (Latin, *quidditas*), in Scholastic philosophy, is the real nature or essence of a thing.

57 l. 8. *demesne*: landed estate (a legal term).

l. 10. *Hall*: probably a guild hall, a place where merchants or tradesmen meet.

l. 12. *most*: i.e. the most, the greatest amount. The phrase sounds as though it were an expression used in playing some game.

Humility. l. 10. *Mansuetude*: gentleness. Each beast, representing one of man's passions, gives a gift to the corresponding but opposed virtue, which can better use that gift.

l. 13. *coral-chain*: the wattle of the turkey; here, an emblem of the flesh.

58 l. 27. *train*: tail-feather.

l. 29. *bandying*: banding together.

l. 31. *amerced*: fined.

l. 32. *Session-day*: a day for 'the sitting together of a number of persons (esp. of a court, a legislative, administrative, or deliberative body) for conference or the transaction of business' (*OED*).

Frailty. l. 9. *Regiments*: methods or systems of governing; but with military overtones fulfilled in l. 23.

l. 11. *sad*: solemn, serious.

l. 13. *weeds*: clothing.

l. 14. *Brave*: showy, ostentatious.

l. 16. *prick*: irritate, inflame.

l. 19. *Affront*: confront, attack.

59 *Constancy*. l. 2. *still*: always.

l. 22. *tentations*: temptations.

l. 33. *To writhe his limbs*. The image is of a bowler who contorts his body to control the ball even after he has released it.

l. 34. *mark-man*: marksman.

60 *Affliction* (III). l. 8. *tallies*: reckonings, accounts.

ll. 10–12. A sigh was apparently believed to shorten life.

61 *The Star*. l. 14. *quickness*: life.

Sunday. l. 11. *worky-days*: working-days.

62 l. 19. *still*: always.

ll. 26–8. *W*'s version of these lines makes the image clearer: 'They are the rows of fruitful trees | Parted with alleys or with grass | In God's rich Paradise.'

l. 40. *took in*: enclosed.

ll. 43–6. Matt. 27: 51, 'and the earth did quake, and the rocks rent.'

l. 47. *Sampson*: Judg. 16: 3, 'And Samson . . . took the doors of the gate of the city [Gaza], and the two posts, and went away with them.'

l. 49. *did unhinge that day*: by removing the day of rest from its position as the seventh day (Gen. 2: 2–3) to its present position as the first day, in commemoration of the Resurrection.

63 ll. 52–6. Rev. 7: 14, 'These are they which came out of great tribulation, and have washed their robes, and made them white in the blood of the Lamb.'

Avarice. l. 7. *fain*: willing (under the circumstances); necessitated, obliged.

64 *To All Angels and Saints.* l. 1. *after all your bands.* As Hutchinson points out, if 'glorious spirits' refers to the 'angels' of the title, then this phrase means 'according to your various ranks'; if, however, the 'glorious spirits' are the redeemed of heaven, the phrase means 'after you have been released from earthly *bonds*'.

l. 5. *yet in his hands.* Isa. 62: 3, 'Thou shalt also be a crown of glory in the hand of the Lord, and a royal diadem in the hand of thy God.'

l. 12. *restorative.* Gold was often used in drugs.

ll. 16–25. Herbert sums up here the Protestant reasons for refusing to engage in prayer to angels and saints for 'special aid' (l. 7): first, because the Bible 'bids no such thing'; and secondly, because 'all worship is [the] prerogative' of God, the ultimate 'power'.

l. 25. *posy:* a bouquet.

65 *Employment* (II). l. 5. *complexions.* A complexion is 'the combination of the four "humours" of the body in a certain proportion, or the bodily habit attributed to such combination' (*OED*).

l. 6. *quick:* live.

ll. 11–15. *Earth* was considered the lowest of the four elements because least active, fire the highest.

l. 20. *Watch:* watch for.

l. 22. *busy plant.* An orange-tree blossoms and bears fruit at the same time.

l. 25. *dressèd:* used here with special reference to the image of the tree; tended, pruned, cultivated.

l. 26. *still too young or old.* We always excuse ourselves as too young or too old to begin.

l. 27. *the Man.* The capitalization in *B* and *W* stresses the general meaning: manhood, maturity, the time when a man might best perform his employment.

66 *Denial.* l. 10. *alarms:* calls to battle.

67 *Christmas.* l. 3. *full cry:* full pursuit: a term from hunting; *cry* refers to 'the yelping of hounds in the chase' or to 'a pack of hounds' (*OED*). Hence the pun on 'dear' (l. 5).

l. 6. *expecting:* waiting.

l. 8. *passengers:* passers-by, travellers.

l. 14. *rack:* frame to hold fodder.

l. 26. See Prov. 20: 27, 'The spirit of man is the candle of the Lord.'

68 *Ungratefulness.* l. 5. *brave:* splendid.

l. 6. Matt. 13: 43, 'Then shall the righteous shine forth as the sun in the kingdom of their Father.'

l. 19. *sweets*. See note on *Church-music*.

69 *Sighs and Groans*. l. 2. *After*: according to, proportionate to. See Ps. 103: 10, 'He hath not dealt with us after our sins; nor rewarded us according to our iniquities.'

l. 5. *silly*: feeble, pitiable, lowly, lacking in good sense.

l. 10. *magazines*: storehouses.

ll. 14–15. *Egyptian night . . . thicken*. Exod. 10: 22, 'and there was a thick darkness in all the land of Egypt three days.'

l. 16. *sewed fig-leaves*. After the Fall, Adam and Eve 'knew that they were naked; and they sewed fig leaves together, and made themselves aprons' (Gen. 3: 7).

l. 20. Rev. 16: 1, 'And I heard a great voice out of the temple saying to the seven angels, Go your ways, and pour out the vials of the wrath of God upon the earth.'

l. 28. *Corrosive*: a medical substance that destroys organic tissue.

70 *The World*. l. 7. *Balconies*: accented *Balcónies*.

l. 11. *Sycamore*: 'a species of fig-tree, *Ficus Sycomorus*, common in Egypt, Syria, and other countries' (*OED*).

l. 14. *sommers*: supporting beams.

Coloss. 3. 3. The full verse from Colossians reads, 'For ye are dead, and your life is hid with Christ in God.'

l. 2. *double motion*. Herbert refers to the 'two motions' of the sun in the Ptolemaic system: its daily ('diurnal', l. 3) route around the earth, and its 'oblique' (l. 4) yearly shifts in the sky.

l. 7. *still*: always.

l. 9. *Quitting*: paying for, paying up.

71 *Vanity* (I). l. 2. *spheres*. In the Ptolemaic system, the planets (including the sun and moon) were thought to move around the earth in nine concentric spheres.

l. 3. *stations*: the points at the extreme limits of a planet's movement where it seems to be standing still.

l. 7. *aspects*: the relative positions of the planets and stars as seen from earth, but also with a pun on the meaning 'face', 'countenance'.

l. 15. *chymick*: an alchemist.   *devest*: unclothe.

72 *Lent*. l. 6. *Corporation*: a legal body 'having authority to preserve certain rights in perpetual succession' (*OED*).

l. 23. *dishonest*: ugly, unseemly; also, shameful, disgraceful.

l. 31. *Christ's fortieth day*: Matt. 4: 1–2, 'Then was Jesus led up of the Spirit into the wilderness to be tempted of the devil. And when he had fasted forty days and forty nights, he was afterward an hungred.'

l. 35. *Be holy ev'n as he*: 1 Pet. 1: 16, 'Be ye holy; for I am holy.'

73 *Virtue*. l. 1. *Sweet*. Again, as in *Church-music*, the poem works with the varied meanings of *sweet*, beginning with the old meaning current in Herbert's day: 'having a pleasant smell or odour; fragrant'. (See also Herbert's poem *The Odour*.) Thus the 'box where sweets compacted lie' of l. 10 implies a box of crushed petals from which fragrant odours arise ('sweets'). Beyond this basic sense the implications move out to include 'agreeable, delightful, charming, lovely' and 'dearly loved or prized, precious, beloved' and from these on to the application of 'sweet' to the soul in l. 13: 'free from offensive or disagreeable taste or smell; not corrupt, putrid, sour, or stale; free from taint or noxious matter; in a sound and wholesome condition' (*OED*).

l. 2. *bridal*: wedding.

l. 5. *angry*. OED suggests: 'having the colour of an angry face: red.'   *brave*: splendid, handsome; but also, in this context, implying a bold and challenging manner.

l. 11. *closes*: with a play on the musical meaning of *close*; a cadence, phrase, or movement—part of a larger composition.

l. 15. *coal*: cinder.

The Pearl. Matth. 13. 45. Matt. 13: 45–6, 'Again, the kingdom of heaven is like unto a merchant man, seeking goodly pearls: Who, when he had found one pearl of great price, went and sold all that he had, and bought it.'

ll. 1–2. Herbert associates the olive press with the printing press.

l. 4. *huswife*: housewife. The old form indicates the pronunciation: 'huzwif' or 'huzzif'.

74 l. 5. *conspire*: unite to produce (by supposed influence upon earthly things).

l. 12. *wit*: cleverness in repartee.

ll. 13–17. *vies*: contests.   *whether party*: which of two parties.

l. 18. *spirit*: alcoholic liquor.

l. 22. *relishes*: pleasures; also, in musical sense, ornaments, embellishments.

l. 26. *unbridled store*: uncontrolled abundance.

l. 32. *sealed*. *W* has *seeled*; the verb 'to seel' means to sew up a hawk's eyelids.

l. 34. *commodities*: material advantages.

l. 37. *labyrinths*: evoking the story of Ariadne.   *wit*: intellect.

l. 38. *silk twist*. This image stems ultimately from the golden chain with which Zeus joins heaven and earth (*Iliad* 8.19–27).

75 *Affliction* (IV). l. 4. *wonder*. Ps. 71: 7, 'I am as a wonder unto many; but thou art my strong refuge.'

l. 12. *pink*: stab, prick, pierce (a fencing term).

76 *Man*. l. 5. *to*: compared to.

l. 8. *more fruit*. The reading of *W*; *B* and *1633* have *no fruit*.

l. 12. *go upon the score*: appear on the account; i.e. they are indebted.

l. 21. *dismount*: bring down.

l. 22. *in little all the sphere*: the entire universe in miniature, the microcosm.

77 l. 34. *kind*: related, but also with the modern meaning.

l. 39. *Distinguishèd*: divided. God's separation of the waters produced dry land, man's 'habitation' (Gen. 1: 9–10).

l. 40. *above*. Above, since rain is necessary to produce food ('meat').

l. 42. *neat*: well-ordered, skilfully made.

l. 50. *brave*: splendid.

l. 52. *wit*: wisdom.

Antiphon (II). See note on *Antiphon* (I).

78 l. 15. *take*: in the elements of Communion.

l. 18. *crouch*: bow down deferentially.

Unkindness. The title has both its modern meaning and that of 'unnatural behaviour'.

l. 1. *coy*: reserved, reluctant.

l. 11. *curious*: elegant, finely made.

l. 14. *thou within them*: Matt. 25: 34–46, especially v. 40, 'Inasmuch as ye have done it unto one of the least of these my brethren, ye have done it unto me.'

l. 16. *pretendeth to a place*: aspires to a political position.

79 *Life*. l. 1. *posy*: bouquet, but also poetry.

ll. 2–3. A parenthetical address to the self, explaining the poem's aim.

l. 3. *band*: the string or other material by which the 'posy' is bound.

Submission. l. 4. *design*: i.e. goal in life.

80 l. 8. *degree*: rank, status.

l. 10. *resume my sight*: 'take back the aims that I had given up'.

l. 12. *Disseize*: dispossess.

Justice (I). l. 1. *skill of*: understand.

l. 9. *mean*: aim at.

l. 10. *the hand*: i.e. the upper hand.

81 *Charms and Knots. Knots*: 'knotty' sayings.

l. 6. *told*: counted.

ll. 15-16. The tithe (one-tenth) paid by the parishioner is repaid by the sermons he hears.

Affliction (V). l. 2. *planted Paradise*: Gen. 2: 8, 'And the Lord God planted a garden eastward in Eden.'

l. 3. *thy floating Ark*. 'The allusion is to the Christian traditional use of the word *Ark*, as in the Baptismal Office, for "the Arke of Christs Church"' (Hutchinson).

82 l. 15. *Some angels*: alluding to the angel who brought the 'good tidings of great joy' at the birth of Christ (Luke 2: 10); and perhaps also to Luke 15: 10, 'there is joy in the presence of the angels of God over one sinner that repenteth'.

l. 17. *sev'ral*: different.   *baits*. Along with the modern sense, *baits* is also used in the old general sense of 'food', while referring specifically to a brief meal served to travellers.   *in either kind*. In the context of 'thy [the Lord's] table' in the next line, this phrase is bound to evoke implications of the two 'kinds' or species of the Communion, that is, the bread and the wine, especially in view of the strong controversy in Herbert's day over whether or not Communion should be served in 'both kinds'. Thus 'our relief' in l. 15 comes to have overtones of reference to Christ, who 'took up' grief in order to accomplish the salvation represented in the Lord's Supper.

l. 22. *curious knots*: intricate flower-beds.   *store*: abundance.

l. 24. *bow*. Both the instrument of God's vengeance and Noah's rainbow (Gen. 9: 11-17), announcing God's covenant.

Mortification. The title indicates the process of decaying along with the practice of 'mortifying the flesh' by meditating on death and human weakness.

l. 2. *sweets*: perfumes.

l. 5. *clouts*: swaddling-clothes.   *winding sheets*: cloths in which to wrap the dead.

83 l. 13. *frank*: free from obligation or worry (the phrase *frank and free* is common).

l. 17. *knell*. As Hutchinson notes, the passing-bell was rung not just after someone had died, but also while he was dying.

l. 18. *befriend him*: by encouraging others to offer prayers for the dying.

l. 24. *attends*: awaits.

l. 32. *solemnity*: a solemn ceremony.

l. 33. *dressed*: prepared.　　　*hearse*: a framework placed over a coffin onto which decorations or verses could be attached.

Decay. l. 1. *Lot*: see Gen. 19: 1–26.

l. 2. *Jacob*: see Gen. 32: 24–30.　　　*Gideon*: see Judg. 6: 11–23.

l. 3. *Abraham*: see Gen. 17: 1–22.

ll. 4–5. See Exod. 32: 7–14, especially vv. 9–10, 'And the Lord said unto Moses, I have seen this people, and, behold, it is a stiff-necked people: Now therefore let me alone, that my wrath may wax hot against them.'　　　*could not | Encounter*: could not go counter to, oppose (Moses' complaint): 'And the Lord repented of the evil which he thought to do unto his people' (Exod. 32: 14).

l. 6. *presently*: at once.

l. 7. God or his messenger appeared to Gideon at an oak (Judg. 6: 11), to Moses in a burning bush (Exod. 3: 2–4), to Elijah in a cave (1 Ks. 19: 9), and to the Samaritan woman at a well (John 4: 6–7).

84 l. 10. *Aaron's bell*. Directions for the making of Aaron's breastplate and robe include the detail, 'a golden bell and a pomegranate, upon the hem of the robe round about' (Exod. 28: 34).

l. 14. *straiten*: confine.

l. 15. *thirds*: a legal term; a widow was entitled to inherit a third of her husband's property at his death.

l. 16. *whenas*: inasmuch as.

Misery. l. 5. *Man is but grass*: Isa. 40: 6, 'All flesh is grass.'

l. 16. *curtains*: i.e. bed-curtains.

ll. 17–18. Ironical, with allusion to various biblical texts that warn against the 'eating' of the moth: Isa. 50: 9, 51: 8; Matt. 6: 19.

85 l. 25. *quarrel*: find fault with.

l. 39. *crouch*: bow reverently.

l. 51. *rug*: blanket, coverlet.

86 l. 62. *winks*: i.e. closes the eyes to something he wishes to ignore.　　　*humours*: the four bodily fluids of the old physiology: blood, phlegm, choler (yellow bile), and melancholy (black bile); without the control of 'knowledge', these physical influences run riot.

l. 69. *posy*: motto, line of poetry. A posy-ring was a ring with an inscription on the inside.

l. 73. *fooled him*: made a fool out of him.

l. 77. *shelf*: reef.

Jordan (II). See the note on *Jordan* (I) for the meaning of the title; the poem is entitled *Invention* in *W*.

l. 3. *quaint*: artful, elaborate.   *invention*: in rhetorical theory, the stage of composition devoted to discovering and developing the subject-matter.

l. 4. *burnish*: spread out, swell.

l. 8. *sped*: successful.

87 l. 10. *quick*: alive, lively.

l. 16. *wide*: wide of the mark.   *pretence*: ambitious effort.

ll. 16–18. These lines (and, in fact, the poem as a whole) echo the first sonnet of Sidney's *Astrophil and Stella*, especially its final line: 'Fool, said my muse to me, look in thy heart and write.' But since this is a recurring theme in Sidney's sequence, other sonnets are also deeply involved. See Sonnet 3, where Sidney scorns the attempts of 'dainty wits' with 'phrases fine' and 'strange similes', and concludes: 'in Stella's face I read | What Love and Beauty be; then all my deed | But copying is, what in her Nature writes.' See also the conclusion of Sonnet 90: 'For nothing from my wit or will doth flow, | Since all my words thy beauty doth indite, | And love doth hold my hand, and makes me write.'

Prayer (II). l. 4. *state*: high rank, powerful position.

l. 9. God joins the earth ('centre') to the outermost sphere of the universe.

l. 15. *fain*: glad.

l. 24. *ell*: a unit of measure (45 inches).

88 *Obedience*. l. 2. *Convey a Lordship*: transfer legal title to a lord's estate.

l. 8. *pass*: convey, transfer legally.

l. 13. *reservation*: a clause in a deed reserving certain rights to the property from being conveyed.

l. 21. *what is man to thee*. Ps. 8: 4, 'What is man, that thou art mindful of him?'

l. 22. *a rotten tree*. Luke 6: 43, 'For a good tree bringeth not forth corrupt fruit; neither doth a corrupt tree bring forth good fruit.'

l. 28. *in earnest*. With a play on the legal meaning of 'earnest': money paid to secure a contract; Christ's sorrows are given 'by way of earnest', as a pledge of salvation to come.

89 l. 42. *kind*: of kindred spirit, along with modern meaning.

l. 43. *Court of Rolls*. The Court of the Master of the Rolls had custody of legal records.

Conscience. l. 12. *physic*: medicine.

l. 13. *receipt*: prescription (for the medicine).

l. 14. *board*: the Communion table, 'God's board', in the ancient phrase preserved in the Prayer Book of Herbert's time.

90 l. 21. *bill*: a halberd.

Sion. l. 2. For the building of Solomon's temple on Mount Zion, see 1 Ks. 5–7.

l. 5. *mystical*: with a secret significance.

ll. 11–12. See Acts 7: 47–8. 'Solomon built him an house. Howbeit the most High dwelleth not in temples made with hands'; and 1 Cor. 3:16, 'Know ye not that ye are the temple of God?'.

l. 21. *quick*: full of life.

91 *Home.* l. 2. *stay*: stay where you are, delay coming, stay away.

l. 15. *without*: outside.

92 l. 37. *meat*: food.

ll. 39–40. *wink | Into.* The primary meaning of 'wink' is 'to close the eyes': one can shut the temptations of the flesh into 'blackness' merely by closing the eyes.

l. 56. *corn*: grain, in British usage.

93 l. 73. *pass not*: do not disregard.

l. 76. *The word is, Stay*: to rhyme with 'pray' (l. 74).

The British Church. It is significant that Herbert does not say 'Anglican', 'English', or even 'Church of England'. *OED* does not record the term 'Anglican' before 1635; it was evidently not in common use in Herbert's day. According to the ancient legend, British Christianity derived directly from Joseph of Arimathea, who came to Britain after Christ's death and established a centre of devotion at Glastonbury. Thus Herbert's title implies a 'British' root for his church, independent of Rome: the church of the ancient Britons.

l. 5. *dates her letters.* Letters were often dated according to holy days; Lady Day (Feast of the Annunciation, 25 Mar.) marked the beginning of the new year, according to the old calendar.

l. 8. *mean*: paltry, shabby.

l. 10. *Outlandish*: foreign.

l. 13. *She on the hills*: Roman Catholicism (on the hills of Rome).

l. 15. *preferred*: advanced (either politically or to heaven).

l. 19. *She in the valley*: Calvinism (Geneva lies in a valley).

94 l. 26. *The mean*: the middle, moderate way.

The Quip. l. 2. *train-bands*: the citizen soldiery of London, the 'trained bands'.

l. 8. The refrain is based on Ps. 38: 15 (BCP): 'thou shalt answer for me, O Lord my God.'

l. 15. *half an eye*: i.e. a glance.

l. 19. *Oration*: perhaps a wry allusion to Herbert's post as Public Orator at Cambridge.

l. 23. *at large*: expansively.

l. 24. *home*: directly, thoroughly, going to the heart of the matter.

95 *Vanity* (II). l. 1. *silly*: simple, naïve.

l. 7. *betimes*: in good time, before it is too late.

l. 11. *mould*: in double sense; pattern, and soil.

The Dawning. Christ's followers came to the tomb on Easter Day 'as it began to dawn' (Matt. 28: 1).

l. 14. *burial-linen.* For the 'linen clothes' and 'napkin' left by Christ in the sepulchre, see Luke 24: 12 and John 20: 5–7.

96 *Jesu.* l. 7. *parcels*: parts, fragments.

l. 9. *I ease you.* I and J were in Herbert's day used interchangeably to indicate both vowel and consonant. In l. 5 'J' must be pronounced as 'I', to rhyme with 'instantly', as Hutchinson notes.

Business. Title: in the basic sense of 'busy-ness'. Such busy activity, forgetting sin, is really idleness. Mankind's true 'business' lies in repentance and remembering Christ's sacrifice.

97 l. 22. *two deaths.* One of the body, the other of the soul in hell; see Rev. 20: 14, 'And death and hell were cast into the lake of fire. This is the second death.'   *fee*: reward, payment.

l. 32. *cross*: misfortune, adversity.

Dialogue. l. 4. *waving.* The old spelling allows two meanings: the old sense of 'wavering' (in one's faith), and the modern 'waiving' (Christ's offer of salvation).

98 l. 9. *balance*: pair of scales.

l. 10. *poise*: a weight used in balancing scales.

l. 20. *savour*: understanding, comprehension.

l. 30. *desert*: pronounced 'desàrt'.

Dullness. l. 3. *quickness*: liveliness.

l. 5. *curious*: elaborate, intricate.

l. 7. *quaint*: elegant, ingenious.

99 l. 12. *red and white.* The colours of ladies' beautiful complexions in courtly love poetry; Herbert had a precedent for an allegorical application to Christ in S. of S. 5: 10, 'My beloved is white and ruddy.'

l. 18. *window-songs*: serenades.

l. 19. *pretending*: courting, wooing.

Love-joy. l. 3. *Annealed*: fixed on (technically, to glass) by a burning process.

l. 8. *JESUS CHRIST*: see John 15: 1, 'I am the true vine.'

100 *Providence*. The poem makes repeated allusions to Ps. 104.

ll. 1–2. Wisd. 8: 1, 'Wisdom reacheth from one end to another mightily: and sweetly doth she order all things.'

l. 9. *fain would*: would like to (this phrase governs 'ditty' as well as 'sing').   *ditty*: compose words for music.

101 l. 39. *temper'st*: tunes.

l. 45. *Tempests are calm to thee*: Matt. 8: 26, 'Then he arose, and rebuked the winds and the sea; and there was a great calm.'

ll. 47–8. Jer. 5: 22, 'Will ye not tremble at my presence, which have placed the sand for the bound of the sea . . . and though the waves thereof toss themselves, yet can they not prevail.'

l. 48. *proud sea*. Job 38: 11, 'and here shall thy proud waves be stayed.'

l. 49. *meat*: food.

l. 51. *their net*: i.e. their mouths.

l. 53. *prevent*: anticipate, come before.

l. 56. *cheer*: provisions, food.

l. 60. *bowls*: bowling-balls (in the English sport), made not quite round, or weighted, so as to run on the 'bias'.

l. 64. *fledge*: feathered.

102 l. 73. *virtue*: power.   *express*: press out, extract; also, describe.

74. *virtues*: inherent powers, especially healing qualities (of herbs) or supposed occult influences (of stones).

l. 85. *Ev'n poisons praise thee*. Poisons often have medicinal qualities.

l. 94. *curious*: involved, complex.

103 l. 97. *good cheap*: at a low price.

l. 126. *The Indian nut*: the coconut.

104 l. 130. *fruits*. Probably the object of 'help', but may be possessive (*fruits'*).

l. 133. *Thy creatures leap not*: i.e. there are no gaps in the chain of being; the gradations between species and kinds are smooth and regular.

l. 144. *owes*: owns.

l. 145. *sev'ral*: different.

l. 146. *advice*: judgement, opinion.

l. 148. *twice*. Both for himself as poet and for the world as its 'high priest' (l. 13).

Hope. See Heb. 6: 19, 'Which hope we have as an anchor of the soul.' Hutchinson offers this explanation: 'The *watch* given to Hope suggests the giver's notion that the time for fulfilment of hopes is nearly due, but the *anchor*, given in return, shows that the soul will need to hold on for some time yet; the *old prayer-book* tells of prayers long used, but the *optick*, or telescope, shows that their fulfilment can only be descried afar off; *tears* receive in return only *a few green eares*, which will need time to ripen for harvest; and then the donor's patience gives out.' The *ring* that the speaker has expected is perhaps a wedding-ring for the bride of Christ (the redeemed soul) at 'the marriage supper of the Lamb' in heaven (Rev. 19: 7–9).

105 *Sin's Round*. l. 2. *course it*: run or gallop about.

l. 4. *cockatrice*. See Isa. 59: 5, where the wicked 'hatch cockatrice' eggs, and weave the spider's web: he that eateth of their eggs dieth.' The cockatrice, or basilisk, is a mythological serpent-like creature that could kill by its glance alone, or by its breath.

l. 8. *the Sicilian Hill*: Mt. Etna.

l. 9. *vent*: expel, but also sell, vend.

l. 10. *ventilate*: increase by blowing; also, make public.

l. 11. *lewd*: bad, evil (but not necessarily lascivious).

l. 15. *As Babel grew*: see Gen. 11: 1–9.

106 *Time*. l. 23. *wants*: lacks.

107 *Gratefulness*. l. 23. *country-airs*: folk-songs.

108 *Peace*. ll. 22–3. *a Prince of old | At Salem dwelt*. See Gen. 14: 18. 'And Melchizedek king of Salem brought forth bread and wine'—a passage interpreted as foreshadowing the elements of the Communion. See also Heb. 6: 20 and 7: 1–2, where Melchizedek is interpreted as the 'type' of Jesus, 'made an high priest for ever after the order of Melchisedec', whose title 'King of Salem' means 'King of peace'.

l. 28. *twelve stalks*: the twelve Apostles.

l. 33. *rehearse*: relate, declare.

l. 34. *virtue*: power, especially 'the power or operative influence inherent in a supernatural or divine being' (*OED*). As the final stanza shows, allusion is made to the Communion service.

109 *Confession*. l. 12. *rheums*: 'watery matter secreted by the mucous glands or membranes' (*OED*).

l. 30. *to*: compared to.

110 *Giddiness*. l. 3. *sev'ral*: different, separate.

l. 11. *snudge*. Herbert seems to draw on two meanings of this word. The first, 'to remain snug and quiet', accords well with the preceding line; the other, 'to be miserly, stingy, or saving' (*OED*), leads to the next line.   *scorns increase*: i.e. scorns to grow in wealth (spends recklessly).

ll. 19–20. As Hutchinson points out, Herbert refers here not to the mammal, but to the mackerel-like fish whose colour changes rapidly when it is removed from the water.

111 *The Bunch of Grapes*. The speaker of the poem parallels his own spiritual situation with the wanderings of the children of Israel in the wilderness: Exod. 13–17. The 'bunch of grapes' refers to the fruit brought back from the Promised Land of Canaan by Moses' spies to demonstrate the land's fertility: Num. 13: 17–25.

l. 4. *vogue*: general course.

l. 5. *air*: manner, mood.

l. 10. *spanned*: measured.

l. 15. *guardian fires and clouds*: Exod. 13: 21, 'And the Lord went before them by day in a pillar of a cloud, to lead them the way; and by night in a pillar of fire, to give them light.'

l. 16. *Our Scripture-dew*. Manna fell with the dew (Exod. 16: 14–15).

l. 17. *shrouds*: temporary shelters, tents.

l. 18. *murmurings*: bitter complaints against God: e.g. Exod. 16: 2–12.

l. 23. *I have their fruit*. See Christ's words in John 15: 1, 'I am the true vine.'

l. 24. *Noah's vine*. Gen. 9: 20, 'And Noah began to be an husbandman, and he planted a vineyard.'

l. 25. *good store*: abundantly.

ll. 27–8. Another allusion to the wine of the Communion, and to its sacramental origin in Christ's blood. See *The Agony*, stanza 2, and Isa. 63: 3, 'I have trodden the winepress alone.'

Love Unknown. This poem depends heavily on a tradition, common to emblem books, of representing the heart as undergoing various afflictions and purifications. The use of the word 'Friend' in the opening line, and again in l. 43, may alert us to the meaning of the dramatic situation: the naïve speaker, it gradually appears, is really talking with his other self—the 'friend' who lives within him, that is, Christ. The suffering of the 'servant' in Isa. 53 was interpreted as a prophecy of Christ's passion.

112 l. 5. *two lives*: a legal mode of land-tenure; the speaker's life in this world and the next.

ll. 12–15. The *fruit* (good works) is of no help toward salvation; only the sacrifice of Christ (the 'rock') has made redemption possible, beginning with baptism (the 'font'); see Herbert's *H. Baptism* (I).

ll. 26–8. *furnace . . . AFFLICTION*. See Isa. 48: 10, 'Behold, I have refined thee, but not with silver; I have chosen thee in the furnace of affliction.'

l. 42. *board*: 'God's board', the Communion table. See Herbert's *Conscience*, ll. 13–15.

113 l. 63. *wot*: know.

l. 66. *quicken*: make lively.

Man's Medley. A 'medley' is any mixture or combination. Herbert calls on two specific senses of the word: a cloth made up of various colours, and 'a musical composition consisting of parts or subjects of a diversified or incongruous character' (*OED*).

l. 8. *pretence*: claim.

114 l. 15. *stuff*: material, cloth.

l. 17. *take place*: assume his rank or station.

l. 18. *After*: according to, in accordance with. *ground*: 'a piece of cloth used as a basis for embroidery or decoration' (*OED*).

The Storm. l. 6. *Amuse*: bewilder, puzzle. This is the reading of *B*; *1633* reads *Amaze*. *object*: place before; i.e. set their crimes before them.

115 l. 7. *storms*: meteor-showers.

116 *The Method*. l. 3. *rub*: in the game of bowls, an obstacle that stopped or diverted the ball.

l. 6. *move*: request, entreat for.

l.8. *he is Love*: 1 John 4: 8, 'For God is love.'

l. 10. *turn thy book*: i.e. turn the pages, look through the 'book' of your soul.

l. 19. *motions*: pleas.

l. 23. *motion*: impulse, inclination.

117 *Divinity*. l. 2. *spheres*: the concentric globes in which the stars and planets were supposed to move in the Ptolemaic system.

l. 11. *jagged*: slashed by way of decoration.

ll. 17–18. Matt. 22: 37–9 and 26: 41; Luke 6: 31.

l. 25. *Epicycles*. In the Ptolemaic system, each planet was thought to move in a small orbit ('epicycle') which had its centre in the circumference of its larger orbit.

118 *Ephes. 4. 30. Grieve not the Holy Spirit, etc.* The entire verse reads, 'And grieve not the holy Spirit of God, whereby ye are sealed unto the day of redemption.'

l. 16. *sense*: capability of feeling, emotional consciousness.

l. 24. *bowels.* In the Bible, the bowels are considered the seat of emotions; see, for instance, Gen. 43: 30, 'And Joseph made haste; for his bowels did yearn upon his brother.' Herbert plays on the fact that lute strings are made of animal gut.

119 l. 31. *still*: always.

l. 36. *store*: abundance.

The Family. l. 14. *Expecting*: awaiting.

120 *The Size.* For the title, compare *The Rose*, l. 4: 'my strict, yet welcome size'. More specifically, a *size* could also mean 'a quantity or portion of bread, ale, etc.', a usage current at Cambridge (*OED*).

l. 4. *passing brave*: surpassingly splendid.

l. 7. *fraught*: freight, cargo.

l. 16. *Exact*: demand, insist upon. This is the reading of *B*; *1633* reads *Enact*.

l. 22. *on score*: on credit.

l. 31. *case*: physical condition, perhaps with a pun on the sense of 'container'.

121 l. 36. *pretender*: suitor.

l. 39. The stanza form indicates that a short line is missing here.

l. 46. *meridian*: 'a graduated ring (sometimes a semi-circle only) of brass in which an artificial globe is suspended and revolves concentrically' (*OED*).

Artillery. l. 2. *Me thoughts*: it seemed to me.

l. 6. *usest*: are accustomed to do.

l. 7. *motions*: impulses, inclinations.

ll. 11–12. Ps. 104: 4, 'Who maketh his angels spirits; his ministers a flaming fire.'

l. 17. *shooters*: shooting stars.

122 l. 31. *articling*: arranging by treaty.

Church-rents and Schisms. l. 1. *rose.* The Church, the 'rose of Sharon' in the traditional interpretation of S. of S. 2: 1.

123 l. 21. *start*: break away from their place.

Justice (II). l. 9. *beam*: the cross-piece from which the dishes of a balance hang.   *scape*: the upright piece of a balance on which the beam is fixed.

l. 10. *engine*: device, machine.

l. 13. *Christ's pure veil*. See Heb. 10: 20, 'the veil, that is to say, his flesh'. This new veil of the Incarnation replaces the veil of the Temple which was rent at the Crucifixion (Matt. 27: 51).

124 *The Pilgrimage*. l. 7. *Fancy's meadow*. A place of worldly delights—in poetry, music, or love. *Fancy*, a contracted form of *fantasy*, is a rich word suggesting works of the creative imagination, a musical *fantasia* (improvization), or amorous attraction.   *strowed*: strewn.

l. 10. *quickened by my hour*: i.e. spurred to action by the consciousness of life's brevity.

ll. 13-15. *wild of Passion ... sometimes rich*. A passage from the *Imitation of Christ* will help to explain these lines: 'when tribulations come, take them as special consolations, saying with the apostle thus: The passions of this world be not worthy of themselves to bring us to the glory that is ordained for us in the life to come' (bk. 2, chap. 12, in the translation by Richard Whitford). *Passion* in l. 13 seems to mean primarily *suffering*, with special allusion to Christ and to what Whitford translates as 'the passions of this world' (Rom. 8: 18, 'the sufferings of this present time'). But the modern meanings of 'passion' are also present, enforced by 'wild', which means 'wilderness', though the adjectival overtones can hardly be avoided. The change to 'wold' recalls localities in England known as 'The Wold', or 'The Wild', or 'The Weald'; the three words or forms were all used to describe what the *OED* defines (under 'wild') as a 'waste place'—that is, a region or tract of land at one time not under cultivation.

l. 17. *Angel*: a gold coin bearing the device of the angel Michael; also, a guardian angel.

l. 36. *chair*: litter, sedan chair.

125 *The Holdfast*. The title and the basic meaning of the poem may be explained by the occurrence of the phrase 'hold fast' in Heb. 4: 14-16, 'Seeing then that we have a great high priest, that is passed into the heavens, Jesus the Son of God, let us hold fast our profession. For we have not an high priest which cannot be touched with the feeling of our infirmities; but was in all points tempted like as we are, yet without sin. Let us therefore come boldly unto the throne of grace, that we may obtain mercy, and find grace to help in time of need.' As Hutchinson notes, the title may also echo Ps. 73: 28 (BCP), 'But it is good for me to hold me fast by God.' One may also recall 1 Thess. 5: 21, 'Prove all things: hold fast that which is good.' The word 'holdfast' was a common workman's term (like 'The Pulley'); it meant

anything that 'binds, supports, or keeps together; *spec.* a staple, hook, clamp, or bolt securing a part of a building or other structure' (*OED*).

ll. 3–10. It is significant that the 'one' who offers all the stern advice in these lines does not appear to be the same as the 'friend' (l. 11) who offers the final consolation.

126 *The Discharge.* A *discharge* is a release from legal obligation.

l. 3. *lickerous*: 'fond of choice or delicious food'; 'having a keen relish or desire for something pleasant'; 'lecherous, lustful, wanton' (*OED*).

l. 8. *with the whole depart*: part with the whole, give it up; also, take leave of, go away from.

l. 21. *fee*: wage, portion.

127 l. 31. *provide*: look into the future.

l. 32. *breaks the square*: i.e. upsets the correct order.

l. 45. *bottom*: a ball of thread or yarn.   *an end*: continuously.

l. 46. *wilt*: wilt thou.

128 *Praise* (II). l. 26. *enrol*: 'record with honour, celebrate' (*OED*).

129 *An Offering.* l. 11–12. See 1 Chron. 21: 17, 'And David said unto God . . . let thine hand, I pray thee, O Lord my God, be on me, and on my father's house, but not on thy people, that they should be plagued.'

l. 22. *All-heal*: a name commonly applied to various plants, because of their supposed medicinal qualities.

130 *Longing.* ll. 8–9. *ground . . . curse.* See God's words to Adam, 'cursed is the ground for thy sake; in sorrow shalt thou eat of it all the days of thy life' (Gen. 3:17).

l. 19. *Bowels of pity.* See Herbert's poem *Ephes. 4.30. Grieve not the Holy Spirit*, note on l. 24.

l. 21. Ps. 86: 1, 'Bow down thine ear, O Lord, hear me.'

131 l. 26. *furnace.* See note on *Love Unknown*, ll. 26–8.

ll. 35–6. Ps. 94: 9, 'He that planted the ear, shall he not hear?'

l. 53. *board*: table; again with the connotation of 'God's board'.

ll. 59–60. *styled | Thy child*: e.g. Rom. 8: 16, 'we are the children of God.'

132 *The Bag.* As ll. 31–2 indicate, the image is that of a bag for letters or dispatches; the stanza-form resembles a bag with handles: a typical piece of Herbertian wit. The image may be related to Job 14: 17, 'My transgression is sealed up in a bag.' The opening line makes clear that the poem is a direct reply to the laments of *Longing*, especially to the prayer of its last stanza. The irregularity of the line-lengths in *Longing* contrasts significantly with the stable stanza-form of *The Bag*.

ll. 2–6. See the story of Christ's calming the tempest, which begins, 'there arose a great tempest in the sea, insomuch that the ship was covered with the waves: but he was asleep' (Matt. 8: 24-7).

133   l. 11. *light*: alight.

l. 13. *tire*: head-dress.

l. 14. *fire*: lightning.

l. 38. *kind*: manner.   *door*. See John 10: 9, 'I am the door: by me if any man enter in, he shall be saved.'

134   *The Jews*. l. 2. *scions*: slips of a plant used for grafting; shoots, twigs.

l. 5. *debtor*. See Gal. 5: 3, where St Paul says the Jew, by rejecting Christ, 'is a debtor to do the whole law'—an impossible obligation.

l. 6. *by keeping lose the letter*. This line depends on St Paul's distinction between spirit and letter; see Rom. 7: 6, 'But now we are delivered from the law, that being dead wherein we were held; that we should serve in newness of spirit, and not in the oldness of the letter.' By attempting to observe the *letter* of the Old Testament law, the Jews lose the New Testament message.

l. 8. *trumpet*. See Joel 2: 1, which was taken to refer to the Last Judgement, 'Blow ye the trumpet in Zion, and sound an alarm in my holy mountain.' It was commonly believed that the conversion of the Jews would take place shortly before the Second Coming.

The Collar. The title contains a pun on 'collar' as an emblem of discipline, and 'choler', yellow bile, the 'humour' causing anger, irascibility. The 'choler' (sometimes spelled 'collar' in Herbert's day) was regarded as a disease; here it implies 'a fit of anger'.

l. 1. *board*. Readers of Herbert's time, and anyone reading *The Temple* in sequence, could hardly avoid the implication that the speaker is striking 'God's board', threatening to leave the Communion table (see *Conscience*, l. 14, *Love Unknown*, l. 42, and *Longing*, l. 53). Hence the ironic echoes of the Communion in ll. 7-12.

l. 6. *still in suit*: always waiting on another, asking favours from another.

l. 9. *cordial*: restorative.

l. 11. *corn*: grain.

l. 14. *bays*: laurels.

135   l. 26. *wink*: close the eyes.

ll. 27-9. *Away, Take Heed ... thy fears*. This reading accepts the argument of Mario Di Cesare (*George Herbert Journal*, 6 (1983), 31) that the text of *B* here is superior to the reading of *1633*: 'Away; take heed: | I will abroad. | Call in thy death's head there: tie up thy fears.' As Di Cesare explains, the speaker is saying, 'Away with such advice as "Take Heed"'—advice 'associated with the skull as object of contemplation'. Beyond this, the words 'take heed' summon up dozens of passages of biblical advice, such as the words of Jesus: 'Take heed therefore that the light which is in thee be not darkness'; or 'Take heed, and beware of covetousness: for a man's life consisteth not in the abundance of the things which he possesseth' (Luke 11: 35; 12: 15). The speaker is casting away all caution, denying the value of all biblical wisdom.

l. 35. *Me thoughts*: it seemed to me.

The Glimpse. l. 6. *Me thinks*: it seems to me.

l. 13. *Lime*: i.e. quicklime, which reacts caustically with water.

136 l. 27. *so that thy stay be short*: 'so that your absence may seem short', or, 'provided that your absence is not greatly prolonged'.

ll. 29–30. 'Do not by thy absence give grief and sin an occasion to jeer at me, whereas *thy coming* would transform my heart into *a court*' (Hutchinson).

Assurance. l. 17. *devils*: treated as one syllable.

137 l. 25. *desert*: merit, deserving; what makes me worthy. The whole stanza alludes to the doctrine that salvation comes only from the 'merits' of Christ, demonstrated in the Crucifixion, and 'imputed' as 'righteousness' to human beings. This is the *league* that Christ has made, 'indited'.

l. 26. *league.* Herbert plays upon the political and military meaning: a 'covenant or compact made between parties for their mutual protection and assistance against a common enemy, the prosecution or safeguarding of joint interests' (*OED*).

l. 29. *indite*: compose, write; perhaps with overtones of *indict*: for by the 'league' Christ condemned himself to death.

l. 35. *my rock and tower.* Ps. 18: 2, 'The Lord is my rock . . . and my high tower.'

The Call. l. 1. John 14: 6, 'I am the way, the truth and the life.'

l. 7. *mends in length*: improves as it progresses.

138 l. 10. *move*: remove. See John 16: 22, 'and your joy no man taketh from you.'

139 *Praise* (III). l. 17. *Pharaoh's wheels.* Exod. 14: 24–5, 'the Lord . . . took off their chariot wheels, that they drave them heavily; so that the Egyptians said, Let us flee from the face of Israel.'

l. 23. *stint*: boundary, limitation.

l. 27. *bottle.* Ps. 56: 8, 'put thou my tears into thy bottle.'

l. 33. *streamers*: flags hung after a victory.

l. 40. *at use*: at interest.   *good store*: abundance.

140 *Joseph's Coat*. For the title, see Gen. 37: 3, 'Now Israel loved Joseph more than all his children . . . and he made him a coat of many colours.' The 'many colours' of the speaker's life are a sign of God's love.

l. 1. *indite*: compose, write.

l. 8. *both*: i.e. 'grief and smart' (one concept) and 'my heart'.

l. 9. *both*: i.e. 'my heart' and 'the body'.   *due*: owed.

l. 11. *ticing*: enticing.

The Pulley. The poem represents a reworking of the myth of Pandora's box. In one version, she opened the box containing all mankind's troubles, which thus made their way into the world, with only Hope remaining in the box; in another version, the box contained all the gods' blessings, which evaporated when she rashly opened it.

l. 5. *span*: the width of an extended hand.

141 *The Priesthood*. ll. 1–3. Refers to the 'power of the keys', which Christ granted to Peter and then to all the disciples; see Matt. 16: 19, 'And I will give unto thee the keys of the kingdom of heaven: and whatsoever thou shalt bind on earth shall be bound in heaven: and whatsoever thou shalt loose on earth shall be loosed in heaven.'

l. 9. *habit*: clothing.

l. 10. *compositions*: 'states of the body, or of body and mind combined' (Hutchinson).

l. 13. *cunning*: skilful.

l. 20. *vessels*. The image of man as a pottery vessel fashioned by God is a biblical commonplace. See, for instance, Jer. 18: 6 and Rom. 9: 20–3.

ll. 25–30. Hutchinson notes, citing the Latin, how closely this stanza seems to echo a passage from the fourth book of the *Imitation of Christ*, the book dealing with the sacrament of Communion: 'O how great and how honourable is the office of priests, to whom is given power to consecrate with the holy words of consecration the Lord of all majesty, to bless him with their lips, to hold him in their hands, to receive him into their mouths, and to minister him to other! O how clean should those hands be, how pure a mouth, how holy a body, and how undefouled should be the heart of a priest, to whom so oft entereth the author of cleanness!' (bk. 4, chap. 11, translated by Richard Whitford).

142 ll. 31–2. See 2 Sam. 6: 6–7, 'Uzzah put forth his hand to the ark of God, and took hold of it; for the oxen shook it. And the anger of the Lord was kindled against Uzzah; and God smote him.'

Ark. The Ark of the Covenant, the wooden chest containing the tables of the law in the Old Testament.

l. 35. *meet*: suitable.

l. 37. *there will I lie.* Walton reports that at Herbert's induction into the priesthood, 'his friend Mr. Woodnot looked in at the church window, and saw him lie prostrate on the ground before the altar' (*Life*, p. 289).

The Search. l. 4. *prove*: prosper, succeed.

l. 7. *centre*: the earth.

l. 14. *Simper*: twinkle.

143   l. 31. *covert*: covering.

l. 33. 'If anything keeps me from you, don't let it be your will that does so.'

l. 47. *charge*: burden.

144   l. 59. *bear the bell*: win first prize.

Grief. l. 10. *a less world*: i.e. man, the microcosm.

145   *The Cross.* A *cross* is any adversity or thwarting of one's aims: the poem's self-irony stems from such biblical texts as Christ's words in Matt. 10: 38, 'And he that taketh not his cross, and followeth after me, is not worthy of me.'

l. 1. *uncouth*: unknown, hard to understand.

l. 12. *threat'nings*: vows.

l. 16. *allowed for*: accepted as; judged to be.

ll. 17–18. 'I am altogether weak except when I contemplate the cross; but its strength spurs me to action' (Hutchinson).

l. 23. *sped*: successfully accomplished.

l. 29. *delicates*: luxuries, delicacies.

146   *The Flower.* l. 3. *demean*: both demeanour and demesne, estate.

l. 11. *blown*: blossomed, bloomed.

l. 16. *quick'ning*: giving life.

l. 18. *chiming*: a harmonious blending of notes.   *passing-bell*: bell rung when someone was dying; as Hutchinson notes, it was a *single* bell and therefore could not *chime*.

147   *Dotage.* l. 2. *Foolish night-fires.* Herbert translates the Latin *ignis fatuus*, the will o' the wisp.

l. 3. *Chases in arras*: representations of hunts (*chases*) on a tapestry (*arras*).

l. 4. *in a career*: i.e. in full career, at full speed.

l. 8. *in grain*: dyed permanently.   *blown*: already blossomed.

148 *The Son.* l. 3. *coast*: region.

A True Hymn. l. 14. *behind*: lacking.

l. 15. *in kind*: i.e. properly (a true hymn).

149 *The Answer.* l. 8. *exhalation*: vapour rising from the ground, regarded as source of a meteor.

l. 9. *means*: aims at.

ll. 13–14. The enigmatic 'answer' or 'reply' seems to depend upon some biblical text such as 'the answer of a good conscience toward God' advised in 1 Pet. 3: 14–21, when people 'speak evil of you': 'But sanctify the Lord God in your hearts: and be ready always to give an answer to every man that asketh you a reason of the hope that is in you with meekness and fear: Having a good conscience.' The 'reason' of course is Christ, and 'the rest' is ultimately Heaven, where those who have come there 'know more than' the speaker can know on earth. (See the 'rest to the people of God' in Heb. 4.)

A Dialogue-Anthem. An *anthem* is a hymn sung antiphonally.

ll. 1–2. 1 Cor. 15: 55, 'O death, where is thy sting? O grave, where is thy victory?'

l. 3. *void of story*: ignorant of history.

l. 6. *Thy curse.* Gal. 3: 13, 'Christ hath redeemed us from the curse of the law, being made a curse for us.'

150 *The Water-course.* l. 8. *sov'reign*: used of medicine to indicate a pre-eminent curative power.

l. 10. *Salvation. Damnation.* The terms are bound to evoke the controversial Calvinist doctrine of 'double predestination'; but Herbert deals with the issue in a characteristically guarded and subtle way. God here gives to man either salvation or damnation 'as he [God] sees fit', not 'according to His Will', as the strict Calvinist would say; 'fit' means 'suitable', 'appropriate'—to what? To what is in God's mind, including, perhaps, consideration of a person's efforts toward virtue and the love of God (aided of course by grace).

Self-condemnation. l. 2. *choosing Barabbas.* See Mark 15: 6–11.

l. 6. *That choice*: i.e. of Barabbas.

151 l. 19. *prevent*: anticipate.

l. 22. *snuffs.* A *snuff* is the portion of a candle-wick that is partly burned away and thus must be removed from time to time.

The Glance. l. 6. *Passing*: surpassing.   *cordials*: restoratives.

l. 7. *embalm*: anoint, with fragrant oil or spices.

152 *The 23d Psalm.* Herbert's version mingles phrasing from three translations of his time: the King James version, the Coverdale version contained in the Book of Common Prayer, and the versified version of Sternhold and Hopkins, whose metre he adopts. He adds the stress on 'love' (ll. 1 and 21), 'And all this not for my desert' (l. 11), 'wine' (l. 19), and the echo of the Song of Solomon in l. 3: 'My beloved is mine, and I am his' (2: 16).

l. 10. *in frame*: into the proper disposition.

l. 24. *thy.* The reading of *B*; *1633* reads *my.*

153 *Mary Magdalene.* For the details of this poem, see Luke 7: 37-50. The identification of this unnamed woman with Mary Magdalene was traditional.

l. 14. *dash*: splash.

Aaron. l. 1-4. For the description of Aaron's garments, see Exod. 28: 4-43.

l. 2. *Light and perfections*: Urim and Thummim, the stones on Aaron's breastplate (Exod. 28: 30).

l. 5. *drest.* The old spelling has here been kept, because of the visual 'rhyme'.

154 ll. 19-20. *old man . . . new drest.* The 'old man' of sin is covered over by the 'imputed righteousness' of Christ.

The Odour. 2. *Cor.* 2. 15. 'For we are unto God a sweet savour of Christ, in them that are saved, and in them that perish.' As Herbert's title indicates, 'savour' is the equivalent of the Greek word for 'smell'; 'savour', like 'sweet', refers here to 'fragrancy' (for Herbert's plays upon the various meanings of 'sweet', see the notes to *Church-music* and *Virtue*).

l. 2. *ambergris*: a secretion of the sperm-whale, used both for cooking and for making perfume.

155 l. 16. *pomander*: a ball of aromatic substances that gives off its scent when squeezed or warmed in the hand (see l. 20).

l. 27. *traffic*: have dealings or relations with one another.

The Foil. A *foil* is a thin leaf of metal placed beneath a gem in order to accentuate its brightness.

The Forerunners. l. 1. *harbingers . . . mark.* Harbingers were those sent in advance to procure lodgings or places for an army or a royal party; they chalked the doors of buildings set aside for royal or military use.

l. 3. *dispark*: turn out of a park (country estate), with a pun on *spark.*

l. 6. *Thou art still my God.* Ps. 31: 14, But I trusted in thee, O Lord: I said, Thou art my God.'

156 l. 9. *pass*: care (again in l. 31).

    l. 11. *ditty*: words for music.

    l. 21. *fond*: infatuated; also, foolish.   *ticed*: enticed.

    l. 26. *arras*: tapestries.

157 *The Rose*. l. 18. *it purgeth*. The flower was used as a laxative.

    l. 29. *physic*: medicine.

158 *Discipline*. l. 22. *a man of war*: Exod. 15: 3, 'The Lord is a man of war.' Cupid, of course, also carried a bow.

159 *The Invitation*. The speaker (apparently a priest) invites 'all' to partake of the Communion 'Banquet'.

    ll. 1–3. These lines, as Hutchinson notes, are reminiscent of Isa. 55: 1–2, 'Ho, every one that thirsteth, come ye to the waters, and he that hath no money; come ye, buy, and eat; yea, come, buy wine and milk without money and without price. Wherefore do ye spend money for that which is not bread?'

    l. 4. *dressed*: made ready (for the service).

    l. 8. *define*: characterize.

    l. 17. *cheer*: food and drink; also gladness, source of joy.

    l. 24. *lower grounds*. Fields were flooded as a means of fertilization.

160 *The Banquet*. For the title see note to *Prayer* (I), l. 1.

    l. 1. *cheer*. See above, note on *The Invitation*, l. 17.

    l. 4. *neatness*: 'elegance of form or arrangement, with freedom from all unnecessary additions or embellishments' (see *OED*, 'neat').

    l. 7. *sweetness*. For Herbert's plays upon the various meanings of 'sweet', see notes to *Church-music* and *Virtue*.

    l. 14. *Made a head*: set up a resistance (literally, raised troops).

    l. 25. *pomanders*. See *The Odour*, l. 16 and note.

161 l. 49. *his*: the reading of *B*; *1633* prints *this*.

    l. 50. *ditty*: words for music; also, theme.

    The Posy. A *posy* is a motto.

    ll. 3–4. This was Herbert's personal motto, which alludes to Gen. 32: 10, 'I am not worthy of the least of all the mercies, and of all the truth, which thou hast shewed unto thy servant'; and to Eph. 3: 8, 'Unto me, who am less than the least of all saints, is this grace given.'

162 *A Parody*. The term *parody* here is derived from the Greek *parodia* ('alongside a song'), a term that had emerged in the late 16th century to describe a common practice of imitation in Renaissance music, especially the transmutation of secular music into sacred music. 'The

essential feature of parody technique is that . . . the whole substance of the source—its themes, rhythms, chords and chord progressions—is absorbed into the new piece and subjected to free variation in such a way that a fusion of old and new elements is achieved' (see the article on 'Parody' in *The New Grove Dictionary of Music and Musicians*). Herbert has performed here a sacred parody by adapting the rhythms, stanzaic form, theme, and some of the words in the following love-song, once attributed to John Donne, but now generally attributed to William Herbert, the 3rd Earl of Pembroke:

> Soul's joy, now I am gone,
> > And you alone,
> > Which cannot be,
> Since I must leave myself with thee,
> And carry thee with me;
>
> Yet when unto our eyes
> > Absence denies
> > Each other's sight,
> And makes to us a constant night,
> When others change to light,
>
> O give no way to grief,
> > But let belief
> > Of mutual love
> This wonder to the vulgar prove:
> Our bodies, not we move.
>
> Let not thy wit beweep
> > Wounds but sense-deep,
> > For when we miss,
> By distance our lip-joining bliss,
> Even then our souls shall kiss.
>
> Fools have no means to meet,
> > But by their feet.
> > Why should our clay
> Over our spirits so much sway,
> To tie us to that way?
>
> O give no way to grief,
> > But let belief
> > Of mutual love
> This wonder to the vulgar prove:
> Our bodies, not we move.

(Spacing is here arranged to fit Herbert's parody; we do not know what manuscript of the love-song Herbert used. He may also have been following music to which the song was set. The text here is based on H. J. C. Grierson's revised edition of Donne's *Poetical Works*, 1933; Grierson notes that one MS reads 'when I am gone' in the opening line.)

163 *The Elixir*. The early version of this poem, in *W*, is entitled *Perfection*. The present title refers to the philosopher's stone, which believers in alchemy thought could turn base metals into gold (see ll. 21–2).

l. 7. *still to make thee prepossessed*: always to place thy claim first.

l. 8. *his*: its (as in l. 15).

l. 15. *tincture*: in alchemy, 'a supposed spiritual principle or immaterial substance whose character or quality may be infused into material things' (*OED*).

l. 23. *touch*: prove genuine by rubbing with a touchstone.

l. 24. *told*: counted.

164 *Death*. l. 1. *uncouth*: strange, not really known; also, with modern sense.

l. 11. *fledge*: i.e. fledged; fully-feathered, able to fly.

165 *Doomsday*. l. 12. *tarantula's raging pains*. 'Tarantism, an hysterical malady, was supposed to be caused by the bite of the wolf-spider or tarantula and to be cured by music and wild dancing' (Hutchinson).

l. 29. *consort*: a group of musicians playing or singing together.

166 *Judgement*. l. 5. *peculiar book*: individual story or book of accounts.

Heaven. There is a long tradition of 'echo' poems, including famous examples by Sir Philip Sidney and by Herbert's brother, Lord Herbert of Cherbury.

l. 19. *persever*. The old spelling indicates the accent: *persèver*.

Love (III). l. 12. See Ps. 94: 9, 'he that formed the eye, shall he not see?'

l. 16. *then I will serve*. But the human speaker is no longer a servant: he is the friend of Love; see Introduction.

ll. 17–18. See Luke 12: 37, 'Blessed are those servants, whom the Lord when he cometh shall find watching: verily I say unto you, that he shall gird himself, and make them to sit down to meat, and will come forth and serve them.' With this text and the preceding poem in the background, the poem evokes the reception of the redeemed at 'the marriage supper of the Lamb' (Rev. 19: 9) as well as the administration of the Communion service.

At the conclusion of *The Church* Herbert has chosen to include poems that deal with only three out of the traditional 'Four Last

Things': Death, Judgement, Hell, and Heaven. He has, character-
istically, substituted Love for Hell, making Love the culmination of
his personal sequence, the climax of his effort to 'copy out only that'.

168 *Poems from Walton's Life.* Walton says the two sonnets were sent to
Herbert's mother 'in the first year of his going to Cambridge . . . for
a New-year's gift', along with a letter from which Walton quotes a
portion in which Herbert writes: 'my meaning (dear Mother) is in
these sonnets, to declare my resolution to be, that my poor abilities
in poetry shall be all and ever consecrated to God's glory' (*Life*, 267–9).
Since we do not know whether Walton here takes the New Year as
beginning on 1 Jan. 1610 or on 25 Mar. we cannot date the occasion
exactly; Herbert would have reached his seventeenth birthday on 3
Apr. 1610.

Sonnet II. l. 14. *discovery*: uncovering, revealing.

Further Reading

EDITIONS

The Works of George Herbert, ed. with introduction and commentary by F. E. Hutchinson (Oxford: Clarendon Press, 1941).

The English Poems of George Herbert, ed. with introduction, bibliography, and notes by C. A. Patrides (London: Dent, 1974).

The Williams Manuscript of George Herbert's Poems. A Facsimile Reproduction, with introduction by Amy B. Charles (Delmar, NY: Scholars' Facsimiles & Reprints, 1977).

The Latin Poetry of George Herbert. A Bilingual Edition, translated by Mark McCloskey and Paul R. Murphy (Ohio State University Press, 1965).

GUIDES TO STUDY

George Herbert: An Annotated Bibliography of Modern Criticism, 1905–1984, compiled by John R. Roberts (University of Missouri Press, 1988).

Essential Articles for the Study of George Herbert's Poetry, ed. John R. Roberts (Hamden, Conn.: Archon Books, 1979). Includes 34 essays and a selective bibliography.

George Herbert: The Critical Heritage, ed. C. A. Patrides (London: Routledge & Kegan Paul, 1983). Selected commentary up to 1936.

George Herbert Journal, ed. Sidney Gottlieb, 1978–. See for current articles and reviews.

A Concordance to the Complete Writings of George Herbert, ed. Mario A. Di Cesare and Rigo Mignani (Ithaca, NY, and London: Cornell University Press, 1977).

BIOGRAPHIES

Charles, Amy M., *A Life of George Herbert* (Ithaca, NY, and London: Cornell University Press, 1977).

Walton, Isaak, *The Life of Mr. George Herbert* (1670), in Walton, *Lives*, World's Classics edn. (London: Oxford University Press, 1927).

STUDIES

Asals, Heather A. R., *Equivocal Predication: George Herbert's Way to God* (University of Toronto Press, 1981).

Benet, Diana, *Secretary of Praise: The Poetic Vocation of George Herbert* (University of Missouri Press, 1984).

Bloch, Chana, *Spelling the Word: George Herbert and the Bible* (University of California Press, 1985).

Bottrall, Margaret, *George Herbert* (London: John Murray, 1954).

Clark, Ira, *Christ Revealed: The History of the Neotypological Lyric in the English Renaissance* (University Presses of Florida, 1982).

Colie, Rosalie L., *Paradoxia Epidemica: The Renaissance Tradition of Paradox* (Princeton University Press, 1966). See esp. chapter 6.

Denonain, Jean-Jacques, *Thèmes et formes de la poésie 'métaphysique'* (Paris: Presses universitaires, 1956).

Edgecombe, Rodney, *'Sweetnesse Readie Penn'd': Imagery, Syntax and Metrics in the Poetry of George Herbert* (Salzburg: Institut, 1980).

Eliot, T. S., *George Herbert*, Writers and their Work, no. 152 (London: Longmans, 1962). Also 'What is Minor Poetry?', in *On Poetry and Poets* (London: Faber & Faber; New York: Farrar, Straus & Giroux, 1957).

Ellrodt, Robert, *L'Inspiration personnelle et l'esprit du temps chez les poètes métaphysiques anglais*, 3 vols. (Paris: José Corti, 1960).

Festugière, A. J., *George Herbert, poète, saint, anglican* (Paris: J. Vrin, 1971).

Fish, Stanley, *The Living Temple. George Herbert and Catechizing* (University of California Press, 1978). Also chapter 3 in *Self-Consuming Artifacts* (University of California Press, 1972).

Freeman, Rosemary, *English Emblem Books* (London: Chatto & Windus, 1948). See chapter 6.

Freer, Coburn, *Music for a King: George Herbert's Style and the Metrical Psalms* (Baltimore and London: Johns Hopkins University Press, 1972).

Gardner, Dame Helen, Introduction to *The Poems of George Herbert*, World's Classics edn. (London: Oxford University Press, 1961). Also *Religion and Literature* (New York: Oxford University Press, 1971).

Grant, Patrick, *The Transformation of Sin: Studies in Donne, Herbert, Vaughan, and Traherne* (Montreal and London: McGill–Queen's University Press; University of Mass. Press, 1974).

Halewood, William H., *The Poetry of Grace: Reformation Themes and Structures in English Seventeenth-Century Poetry* (New Haven and London: Yale University Press, 1970).

Harman, Barbara Leah, *Costly Monuments: Representations of the Self in George Herbert's Poetry* (Cambridge, Mass., and London: Harvard University Press, 1982).

Hodgkins, Christopher, *Authority, Church, and Society in George Herbert: Return to the Middle Way* (University of Missouri Press, 1993).

Knights, L. C., 'George Herbert', in *Explorations* (London: Chatto & Windus, 1946).

Leishman, J. B., *The Metaphysical Poets* (Oxford: Clarendon Press, 1934).

Lewalski, Barbara Kiefer, *Protestant Poetics and the Seventeenth-Century Religious Lyric* (Princeton University Press, 1979).

Low, Anthony, *Love's Architecture: Devotional Modes in Seventeenth-Century English Poetry* (New York University Press, 1978).

Mahood, M. M., *Poetry and Humanism* (New Haven, Conn.: Yale University Press, 1950). See chapter 2. Also 'Something Understood: The Nature of Herbert's Wit', in *Metaphysical Poetry*, ed. Malcolm Bradbury and David Palmer, Stratford-upon-Avon Studies no. 11 (London: Edward Arnold, 1970).

Maleski, Mary A., Ed. *A Fine Tuning: Studies of the Religious Poetry of Herbert and Milton* (Binghamton, NY: Medieval & Renaissance Texts & Studies, 1989).

Manley, Frank, 'Toward a Definition of Plain Style in the Poetry of George Herbert', in *Poetic Traditions of the English Renaissance*, ed. Maynard Mack and George deForest Lord (New Haven and London: Yale University Press, 1982).

Martz, Louis L., *The Poetry of Meditation* (New Haven: Yale University Press, 1954; second edn. with new preface and revised conclusion, 1962). Also *From Renaissance to Baroque* (University of Missouri Press, 1991). Contains two essays on Herbert.

Miller, Edmund, and DiYanni, Robert, eds., *Like Season'd Timber: New Essays on George Herbert* (New York: Peter Lang, 1987).

Miner, Earl, *The Metaphysical Mode from Donne to Cowley* (Princeton University Press, 1969).

Rickey, Mary Ellen, *Utmost Art: Complexity in the Verse of George Herbert* (University of Kentucky Press, 1966).

Roberts, John R., ed., *New Perspectives on the Seventeenth-Century English Religious Lyric* (University of Missouri Press, 1994). Includes a fifty-page 'Selective Bibliography of Modern Criticism'.

Ross, Malcolm Mackenzie, *Poetry and Dogma: The Transfiguration of Eucharistic Symbols in Seventeenth-Century English Poetry* (New Brunswick, NJ: Rutgers University Press, 1954). See chapters 6 and 7.

Schoenfeldt, Michael C., *Prayer and Power: George Herbert and Renaissance Courtship* (University of Chicago Press, 1991).

Seelig, Sharon Cadman, *The Shadow of Eternity: Belief and Structure in Herbert, Vaughan and Traherne* (University Press of Kentucky, 1981).

Shaw, Robert B., *The Call of God: The Theme of Vocation in the Poetry of Donne and Herbert* (Cambridge, Mass.: Cowley Publications, 1981).

Sherwood, Terry G., *Herbert's Prayerful Art* (University of Toronto Press, 1989).

Stein, Arnold, *George Herbert's Lyrics* (Baltimore: The Johns Hopkins Press, 1968).

Stewart, Stanley, *George Herbert* (Boston: Twayne Publishers, 1986).

Strier, Richard, *Love Known: Theology and Experience in George Herbert's Poetry* (University of Chicago Press, 1983).

Summers, Claude J., and Pebworth, Ted-Larry, (eds), *'Too Rich to Clothe the Sunne': Essays on George Herbert* (University of Pittsburgh Press, 1980).

Summers, Joseph H., *George Herbert: His Religion and Art* (London: Chatto & Windus; Cambridge, Mass.: Harvard University Press, 1954; reprinted Binghampton, NY: Medieval & Renaissance Texts & Studies, 1981).

Sister Thekla, *George Herbert, Idea and Image: A Study of The Temple* (The Greek Orthodox Monastery of the Assumption, Filgrave, Newport Pagnell [now Normanby, Whitby], 1974).

Todd, Richard, *The Opacity of Signs: Acts of Interpretation in George Herbert's 'The Temple'* (University of Missouri Press, 1986).

Toliver, Harold, *George Herbert's Christian Narrative* (Pennsylvania State University Press, 1993).

Tuve, Rosemond, *A Reading of George Herbert* (University of Chicago Press; London: Faber & Faber, 1952). Also 'George Herbert and *Caritas*' and 'Sacred "Parody" of Love Poetry', in *Essays by Rosemond Tuve*, ed. Thomas P. Roche, Jr. (Princeton University Press, 1970).

Vendler, Helen, *The Poetry of George Herbert* (Cambridge, Mass., and London: Harvard University Press, 1975).

Warnke, Frank J., *Versions of the Baroque* (New Haven and London: Yale University Press, 1972).

White, Helen C., *The Metaphysical Poets: A Study in Religious Experience* (New York: Macmillan, 1936). See chapters 6 and 7.

Index of Titles and First Lines

OXFORD

MORE OXFORD PAPERBACKS

This book is just one of nearly 1000 Oxford Paperbacks currently in print. If you would like details of other Oxford Paperbacks, including titles in the World's Classics, Oxford Reference, Oxford Books, OPUS, Past Masters, Oxford Authors, and Oxford Shakespeare series, please write to:

UK and Europe: Oxford Paperbacks Publicity Manager, Arts and Reference Publicity Department, Oxford University Press, Walton Street, Oxford OX2 6DP.

Customers in UK and Europe will find Oxford Paperbacks available in all good bookshops. But in case of difficulty please send orders to the Cash-with-Order Department, Oxford University Press Distribution Services, Saxon Way West, Corby, Northants NN18 9ES. Tel: 0536 741519; Fax: 0536 746337. Please send a cheque for the total cost of the books, plus £1.75 postage and packing for orders under £20; £2.75 for orders over £20. Customers outside the UK should add 10% of the cost of the books for postage and packing.

USA: Oxford Paperbacks Marketing Manager, Oxford University Press, Inc., 200 Madison Avenue, New York, N.Y. 10016.

Canada: Trade Department, Oxford University Press, 70 Wynford Drive, Don Mills, Ontario M3C 1J9.

Australia: Trade Marketing Manager, Oxford University Press, G.P.O. Box 2784Y, Melbourne 3001, Victoria.

South Africa: Oxford University Press, P.O. Box 1141, Cape Town 8000.

OXFORD POETRY LIBRARY
ANDREW MARVELL
Edited by Keith Walker and Frank Kermode

Marvell is regarded as one of the finest Metaphysical poets. His brilliant use of conceits and luxuriant imagery is ever-present in this selection which includes much of his lyrical poetry together with some of his more political works. Such famous poems as *To his Coy Mistress*, the Mower poems, and *On a Drop of Dew* can all be found, with informative notes and introduction by Frank Kermode and Keith Walker.

ANTHONY TROLLOPE IN THE WORLD'S CLASSICS

THE THREE CLERKS

Anthony Trollope

Edited with an Introduction by
Graham Handley

The Three Clerks is Trollope's first important and incisive commentary on the contemporary scene. Set in the 1850s, it satirizes the recently instituted Civil Service examinations and financial corruption in dealings on the stock market.

The story of the three clerks and the three sisters who become their wives shows Trollope probing and exposing relationships with natural sympathy and insight before the fuller triumphs of Barchester, the political novels, and *The Way We Live* Now. The novel is imbued with autobiographical warmth and immediacy, the ironic appraisal of politics and society deftly balanced by romantic and domestic pathos and tribulation. The unscrupulous wheeling and dealing of Undy Scott is colourfully offset by the first appearance in Trollope's fiction of the bullying, eccentric, and compelling lawyer Mr Chaffanbrass.

The text is that of the single-volume edition of 1859, and an appendix gives the most important cuts that Trollope made for that edition.

THE OXFORD AUTHORS

General Editor: Frank Kermode

THE OXFORD AUTHORS is a series of authoritative editions of major English writers. Aimed at both students and general readers, each volume contains a generous selection of the best writings—poetry, prose, and letters—to give the essence of a writer's work and thinking. All the texts are complemented by essential notes, an introduction, chronology, and suggestions for further reading.

Matthew Arnold
William Blake
Lord Byron
John Clare
Samuel Taylor Coleridge
John Donne
John Dryden
Ralph Waldo Emerson
Thomas Hardy
George Herbert and Henry Vaughan
Gerard Manley Hopkins
Samuel Johnson
Ben Jonson
John Keats
Andrew Marvell
John Milton
Alexander Pope
Sir Philip Sidney
Oscar Wilde
William Wordsworth